The Appaloosa

By Bill and Dona Richardson

The Appaloosa grew naturally as a result of the fact that Mr. and Mrs. Richardson — who are longtime breeders of the spotted horses — were constantly being made aware of the pressing need for a book that would answer questions from both newcomers and established breeders about this very popular horse.

The Appaloosa horse can be traced back through history to the Ice-Age cave-dwellers of Central Europe, whose paintings include several examples of horses that bear the unmistakable Appaloosa markings. The breed's popularity in recent years has caused their numbers to grow so rapidly that the gaily patterned horses now constitute the third-largest breed registry in the entire world.

In this lively, fast-paced, no-nonsense book there is much information both for those who are entirely new to the world of horses and for those more experienced hands, who are nevertheless unfamiliar with this particular breed.

You will first be given a short summary of the horse's fascinating history; then you will learn the characteristics that identify an Appaloosa (his famous spotted markings make this easy), and pointers on how to buy and how to breed Appaloosas.

Of course you will want to show him, and complete information is given on the various kinds of shows and classes, how to prepare your horse for his performance, and — perhaps most helpful of all — the Richardsons have supplied a complete rundown on the qualities that judges especially look for.

You will certainly want to examine the chapter on the Appaloosa's remarkable versatility, which the authors consider to be the key to his popularity, and the chapters on the Appaloosa Horse Club and the Appaloosa registration system. Included here are specimen applications for registration and complete explanations of the rules pertaining to registration requirements. Information about the club and its activities also make it interesting for would-be members.

Not only an excellent reference book, *The Appaloosa* is certain to entertain those who are merely interested in horses, but who have no desire — or room — to breed or show them. They will take special delight in the large number of photographs, which show the Appaloosa — as a foal and as a mature horse; in the field, in the show ring, and hard at work; and as an inspiration for works of art in many diverse cultures and ages.

The spotted horse has been a friend to man throughout the animal's long and colorful history, and as the authors point out, "he is still proving his worth to those fortunate enough to own him today — in show rings, on working ranches, on the pleasure trails, on the race tracks, and as a good companion to the many thous? of people who love horses."

Cover photograph

High Bar – Grand Champion Appaloosa Stallion
Owned by Jim & Gabe Duque

Standing at stud at
The Bar D Bar Ranch
Star Route 192
Hemet, California

THE APPALOOSA

by
**Bill and Dona
Richardson**

Melvin Powers
WILSHIRE BOOK COMPANY
12015 Sherman Road
No. Hollywood, California 91605

ISBN 0-87980-182-4
Printed in the United States of America

Preface

Although nearly unknown to most horsemen only a few years ago, the Appaloosa now ranks as one of the top horse breeds in the world. He has captured the hearts, admiration and interest of people everywhere, and this has caused a flurry of questions to be raised concerning his origin, technical descriptions, points of judging and other pertinent facts.

Although the Appaloosa can be traced back into the dawn of history, it has only been in comparatively recent years that the modern world of horsedom has discovered him. Registered Appaloosas now comprise the third largest breed registry in the world, and it is still growing! This rapid increase in popularity has created a need for a concentrated source of information on the Appaloosa, and it is for this purpose that *The Appaloosa* has been written.

Some of the material contained in these pages has been designed to answer questions for those who might be new to the world of horses in general; some has been aimed at instructing those who are new only to Appaloosas. No one likes to be classified as a "dude"; we all would prefer to be looked upon as experts. Perhaps some of the information presented here will help a few readers to make a step toward the expert status through acquisition of new knowledge.

The focal point of this manuscript is of course the Appaloosa horse. Although some chapters touch lightly on the subject of handling a horse properly in certain given situations, it has not been the intention of the authors to enter the field of training as such. There are many fine books written on training by those much more competent to write them. The few tips and suggestions presented here are just simple aids that someone might find useful.

No book on the Appaloosa would be complete without historical references and information on the breed's origin. These historical facts might still be matters of mystery, were it not for the efforts of Francis Haines in researching the subject both at home and abroad.

The authors would like to extend their deepest gratitude to those who have given encouragement and assistance throughout the preparation of this book. Special thanks go to George B. Hatley, Executive Secretary of the Appaloosa Horse Club, Calvin Briley, whose untimely death prevented him from seeing the finished work, and Claude Thompson, founder of the breed registry, for his support and approval. To these men, and to all Appaloosa people everywhere, this book is humbly dedicated.

Contents

THE APPALOOSA

1

Some Appaloosa History

The Appaloosa is the oldest identifiable breed of horse still in existence today. Ancient sketches found on the walls of Ice Age caves of central Europe, estimated to be some 20,000 years old, show several examples of horses that bear the unmistakable spotted markings of the Appaloosa. Man had not yet learned to use the horse for anything but a source of food at that period of history, so it is assumed that the artistic caveman eventually ate his models for supper. Regardless of one's feelings toward him on this point, we are indebted to him for his drawings.

Many works of art created throughout the centuries that followed the retreat of the icy glaciers provide undeniable proof of the existence of the spotted horse in many parts of the world. A scabbard dating from approximately 1000 B.C. and decorated with horses bearing the characteristic Appaloosa coat pattern was found in Austria. Chinese art, including vases and wall hangings that date to 500 B.C., have horses in their designs that clearly show the singular elliptical Appaloosa spots scattered over their rear quarters. Paintings, carvings, writings in legends and poetry, children's toys and household articles which deal with or are adorned with spotted horses have all been found. Greek history records a great breed of war horse that was used by the Persians *circa* 480 B.C., which is clearly described as an Appaloosa.

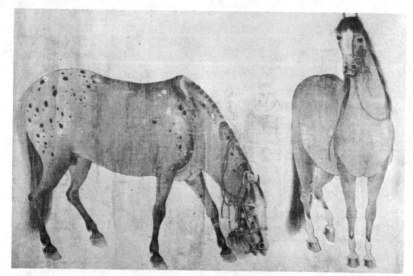

Chinese silk wall hanging circa 1280 A.D. (Courtesy of Fogg Museum)

At the time when the Great Wall was actively being attacked by the fierce tribes from the north, the Chinese armies had only the small Northern Mountain Pony as a means of transportation. This pony, still native to the region of Mongolia today, was short on endurance, suffered a variety of foot ailments, and was very unsatisfactory for use as a cavalry animal. Hearing about the Persian war horses with the spotted coats, Emperor Wu Ti of China was determined to obtain them for his own army. Reports finally came to him of a small, remote valley located in the interior of the continent where these horses were to be found. The Emperor began a campaign to acquire these animals that lasted twenty-five years and cost the lives of thousands of Chinese people. When his initial efforts to procure the horses were rebuffed, he launched an all-out military campaign and eventually did secure a sufficient number to satisfy his needs. Ballads, silk hangings and many other works of art dating from this period and now owned by museums depict these "Heavenly Horses" of China that we call Appaloosas today.

Through the ensuing years, the Appaloosa found himself in northern France in the year 1600 A.D., where he enjoyed much favor by members of the court of King Louis XVI as a saddle

Ancient Chinese figure clearly shows the characteristic spots of the Appaloosa.

Several paintings by central European artists of the seventeenth and eighteenth centuries. Appaloosas were very popular with royalty during this period.

The Roan Horse. This painting, by Paulus Potter in 1630, hangs in The Louvre in Paris, France.

horse and as a coach horse. In 1685, a horse known as "Bloody Buttocks" was imported into England, and although the information about this animal is somewhat vague and sketchy, he is believed to be the first Appaloosa to be brought into that country. Through the years, the spots on the Appaloosas were sometimes called "blood spots," stemming from ancient times when superstitious observers thought the spots were the result of the horse sweating blood. This would account for the English horse's unusual name.

Thousands of centuries ago, a form of small horse was native to the North American Continent. Some unknown force of nature caused this animal to become extinct, so that the horses brought to the New World by the Spaniards during the sixteenth century were sources of wonder to the native population. Two horses brought in the original group are thought to have been Appaloosas; without a doubt succeeding trips included more of the spotted horses, and these became the nucleus of what would grow into the entire Appaloosa population of the Western Hemisphere.

The Indians were fascinated by this amazing animal that carried men easily, transported heavy goods over rough country and served as an effective weapon for military purposes. They had been accustomed to using dogs to carry their possessions by fastening a travois to their shoulders and letting the other ends drag behind, while a hide across the two formed the carrier. Hunting and warring parties stalking game—even buffalo—and made warring raids on other tribes, all on foot. The huge beasts of the Spaniards were frightening at first, but this soon dissolved into respect and a desire for ownership.

It was common for the conquering Spaniards to use native Indian boys and men to help them with their work, which included care of their horse herds. No doubt some of these lads "borrowed" a few of the Spanish horses from time to time, although at great personal risk. Some of the animals would occasionally break free on their own, and once lost in the nearby hills they were rarely recovered. From these few individuals, large wild herds of horses were produced that roamed all over

Very old (date unknown) photo of two Indian women mounted on an Appaloosa, taken about the time of the Klamath Indian wars.

the central and western United States during the seventeenth and eighteenth centuries, providing the American Indian with a new and very useful form of life.

In a slow migration from Mexico, horses eventually found their way into the northwestern region of the country by about 1730. Among these were a number of the spotted horses which would soon receive the new name, Appaloosa.

The Palouse country, where the modern Appaloosa horse was developed, lies in parts of Eastern Washington, Northeastern Oregon, and the Idaho panhandle. For the most part it is open and gently rolling country, with a hot, dry climate in the summer, and a cold, dry climate in winter. The mighty Snake and Columbia Rivers flow through here, as well as many smaller streams including the Palouse River. The hills are a rich, golden color in summer as the native grasses cure in the warm sun.

In the southeast corner of this land is the Grand Ronde Valley, where the Nez Perce Indians lived, hunted and raised their beautiful horses on the rich forage that the Valley provided. Tall, majestic snow-capped Wallowa Mountains, their slopes covered with thick timber and dotted with small, crystal-clear lakes, protectively circle this pasture-land, forming a natural corral for the thousands of Appaloosa horses grazing below.

This was the home of the Nez Perce, a highly developed Indian tribe that had been practicing selective breeding of Appaloosas for many generations before the white man came to this country. Carefully selecting top mares and outstanding stallions to keep for breeding stock, the Indians gelded or traded all inferior animals to other tribes.

To the Indian, "the best" in horseflesh meant the animals that were swiftest and surest of foot. But it also meant more in that open country where there were no corrals or fences. The Indian needed a horse which was gentle enough to allow his rider to walk up to him in open country and climb aboard without nonsense. Particularly when hunting and warring, the horse that was hard to control, or was flighty in critical moments, was a poor choice of mount and could cost his owner his life. A horse that spooked from the sign of bear, elk or buffalo made it impossible for the hunter to get close enough for a kill.

The only means used by the Nez Perce to control their horses while riding them was a rawhide thong tied around the lower jaw of the animal just loose enough so it didn't bother him or hurt his mouth, but tight enough to provide control and stay in place. The end reached up around the horse's neck for a rein. The Indian rode bareback, and to hunt with a bow and arrow meant both hands of the rider had to be free to use the weapon while the horse moved at a full gallop over rough country, changing direction suddenly and often. At these times, knee action was the rider's only means of control. Such horses were the results of good breeding and some good training, and a lot of natural ability.

Jesse Redheart, Nez Perce Indian, rides the Appaloosa "Freel's Chico" through the land of Chief Joseph.

Nez Perce Indians were well-acquainted with the qualities of the Appaloosa horse.

The Indian was quick to learn that just any old horse wouldn't always respond to training. In order to be trained for the needs of the Indian, a horse had to have a certain willingness to learn, and had to develop a certain loyal attachment or preference for his owner. Call it "love" or "affection" or whatever you please, the Appaloosa has a lot of it. It's a feeling that blossoms early when a man and an Appaloosa find each other, and it's made up, among other things, of tenderness, confidence, dependence and independence. The Nez Perce recognized this quality in their Appaloosas, and prized it very highly.

Buffalo Bill's sister used to tell stories about her famous brother and his Appaloosa horse, which was trained to come when Bill whistled for him. This was more than an amusing trick; it was a very useful way to catch a horse in open country. Not all horses have the disposition or inclination to learn something of this nature, but it was common for the Indian to train his Appaloosa this way.

To an Indian, a horse meant wealth. The more horses he owned, the more things he could buy. Just as we today have money of different denominations, the Indian had horses of different values. The most prized horse was the one that not only was dependable and easy to train, but in addition carried a snow-white blanket in which dollar-sized dark spots were scattered over his rump. Sometimes these spots were arranged by Nature into a handprint design, and the Nez Perce warrior who owned a magnificent horse like this was the proudest and richest Indian of them all!

The Appaloosa horse has been known by many names throughout the ages. The Appaloosa *breed* is not new; the *name* is. White settlers and Army men, traveling through the Palouse River country, took note of the swift, well-made Indian horses with the loud markings, and called them "a Palouse horse." The name "A Palousy" or "Appaloosie" was used to distinguish them from the mustangs, pintos, paints, and solid-colored horses used by other Indian tribes.

In their Journals, Lewis and Clark indicated they were very favorably impressed with the Nez Perce Indians, considering them to be one of the most colorful of all the tribes they had

Staged version of an Indian meeting a Mountain Man. Both used and respected the Appaloosa horse.

This young Indian girl and her Appaloosa are a colorful sight.

contacted. The beadwork and designs found on Nez Perce robes and garments were so unusual that several buffalo robes having stories painted on them were brought back as gifts for President Jefferson. These are now in the possession of the Smithsonian Institution.

For a people who enjoyed decorating their clothing, robes and wikiup homes, it was only natural that they would also prefer a "decorated" horse. Lewis and Clark found huge herds of beautiful spotted horses in the Nez Perce land, which they described as being "equal to and surpassing anything we had seen in the pastures of Virginia."

In 1877, the Nez Perce owned many thousands of outstanding Appaloosa horses. Rather than give up the land where his people had lived so long and where the bones of his father were buried, Young Chief Joseph led his Nez Perce warriors into victory after victory over the United States Army. The Indians out-ran, out-fought and out-maneuvered the commands of four of the Army's most experienced Indian fighting generals. By their own accounts, these men have admitted that if it hadn't been for the telegraph, the Army's superior numbers and Chief Joseph mistakenly believing he was safely over the Canadian border, the Nez Perce would have won the freedom they fought so hard to attain.

During the long, weary, battle-scarred march from their homeland to just north of the Bear Paw Mountains in Montana—a distance of 1,800 miles— the Nez Perce fought and traveled, taking their women, children, homes and horses with them the entire way. Their warriors numbered just under 300 at the start, but eleven engagements with U. S. Troops, of which five were major battles, took their toll in death. Believing that the Missouri River marked the Canadian border and safety, Chief Joseph stopped to rest his tired band. Only 87 warriors remained from the original force, and 40 of these were wounded. They were engaged by the enemy, and received their first defeat of the campaign. They had come so far, fought so hard, and suffered so much; they had not the strength nor the warriors to fight again in a war they now recognized was hopeless. A light snow had started to fall, but the sun shone that October day in 1877 when Chief Joseph surrendered his starving band to General O. O. Howard, and delivered his now-famous speech that ends, "Now hear me, oh my chiefs. I am tired. My heart is sick and sad. From where the sun now stands, I will fight no more forever."

The Appaloosa horse herd so carefully built by the Nez Perce tribe became an object for deliberate annihilation by the Army on written orders to kill or destroy every Appaloosa which could be found. Never in history has such a useful member of Nature's kind been the target for such a cold-blooded slaughter as took place with the Appaloosa at the close of the Nez Perce War of 1877. In one recorded incident, 400 head of choice Appaloosa stock were driven into a ravine while men with Army rifles on the banks above fired into the frightened mass of horseflesh in the death trap until not one horse remained alive. Thousands of others were caught and destroyed singly and in small groups until the breed was reduced to the few that managed to flee to the meadows and high valleys of the mountains, and the handful "requisitioned" by cavalry officers who knew their quality.

It is easy to imagine the state of minds of the soldiers who carried out these grisly orders. Only one year previously, in southeastern Montana, Lt. Col. George A. Custer had suffered a humiliating defeat at the hands of the Indian. More recently, the battles with the Nez Perce in which the Army was consistently defeated were fresh wounds in their injured vanities. They had seen what the Nez Perce could do when mounted on their amazing spotted horses, and hatred fanned their determination that no Indian would ever be able to use such animals in war again. Clearly, without horses, the Indian could no longer war or hunt or gamble or in any way continue to live the free, happy life he had always known. The answer was given: take away the weapons and horses of the Indian, and it would then be easy to turn him toward the more peaceful activities of farming.

Local missionaries, in their zeal to gather religious converts, heartily endorsed and aided this plan. Without horses, the Indian would be a much more subdued sinner to teach. But without horses, the Indian could not farm. So a compromise was reached. The Indian would be allowed horses of draft stock for their use; any Appaloosas that might still be owned by the Indians would have to have draft blood infused in their foals, or be shot. Recognizing that a draft horse makes a seriously inferior mount for racing or hunting, they felt the problem was solved.

Perhaps so. The heart of the Nez Perce that had taken him through so many battles and so many miles was irreparably broken with the bodies of his magnificent spotted horses. His surrender was complete, and he never again rode the warpath.

Although a handful of Appaloosas escaped destruction at the hands of the Army, and lived to produce more of their beautiful spotted kind in the high mountain country, the largest majority were killed or bred to draft stock. Exactly sixty years later, in 1937, there remained only a few hundred known domesticated representatives of this famous breed in the entire world.

A magazine article concerning the tide that was sweeping this proud breed toward extinction inspired Claude Thompson of Moro, Oregon, to set the machinery in motion that was to save the Appaloosa from being lost for all time. As the result of the efforts of this man and those who followed him, the Appaloosa has once again risen in popularity and numbers to become one of the most desired breeds of horses in the world today, and for the same reasons he was so sought after by Emperor Wu Ti, the Persians, the Spaniards and the American Indian: his durability, intelligence, outstanding performance as a rough-country horse, and his ever delightful beautiful spotted coat. The Appaloosa is still proving his worth to those fortunate enough to own him today— in show rings, on working ranches, on the pleasure trails, on the race tracks, and as a companion to the many thousands of people who love horses.

2
How To Spot An Appaloosa

Because of his peculiar color patterns, the Appaloosa is perhaps the easiest breed of horse to identify, close-up or at a distance. Some individuals carry what is known as a "marginal" color pattern, and these animals may require the eye of an expert for identification; but for the most part, the loud blankets and varied patterns of spots sported by the greatest number of Appaloosas make it a lot easier to identify a field of these horses than, say, a field of solid-colored Quarter Horses or Morgans.

The quality of the animal is always the prime consideration and color patterns should never be used as the only means of identifying an Appaloosa. The white sclera in the eye, striped "laminated" hooves and mottled skin should always be sought as identifying Appaloosa characteristics. But it cannot be denied that without one of the characteristic coat patterns, an Appaloosa is not an Appaloosa anymore than a steer could be called a Hereford without the well-known red-and-white markings of that breed of cattle.

On December 24, 1950, the National Association of Stallion Registration Boards issued its acceptance of the Appaloosa horse as a recognized breed, thereby officially establishing the Appaloosa as a type and conformation as well as color pattern. The Appaloosa Horse Club, Inc. of Moscow, Idaho, has issued a detailed descrip-

The sparse rat-tail of the Appaloosa is very evident on this animal.

tion of the basic conformation of the Appaloosa which, in brief, demands that his general appearance be that of a good riding horse with a straight and lean head, wide forehead, prominent eye, deep chest, medium pointed ears, short cannons, long, sloping pasterns, muscular thighs, quarters and gaskins. Generally speaking, this describes the basic conformation of any good light horse. In addition, however, the Appaloosa characteristics are added: parti-colored skin about the nostrils, lips and reproductive organs; white sclera in the eye; a prominent, well-defined wither; and, of course, one of the prescribed color patterns. The animal must show quality, refinement and balance throughout, with most Appaloosas ranging from 950 to 1175 pounds at an average height of 14:2 to 15:3 hands. Minimum height for registration is 14 hands.

Not required for registration but often a secondary characteristic of the breed is a sparse mane and tail (sometimes called "rat-tail"), and one or more striped hoof. Anyone who is accustomed to the full, flowing tails of the Palomino or the American Saddlebred will find the rather skimpy points of an Appaloosa a certain contrast, perhaps even unattractive. However, this was a basic characteristic of the original Appaloosa, and while those animals being bred for the show ring tend more toward the fuller mane and tail, the rat-tail is more indicative of Appaloosa heredity.

The white sclera in the eye of an Appaloosa tends to give him an alert appearance. It resembles the human eye, which is also encircled with a similar white substance. Many old-time horsemen, and some modern ones too, believe that a horse which shows the white sclera is just naturally mean and wild. While many horses of all breeds will show the white around their eyes when frightened, it is erroneous to believe this is a characteristic of flighty or spooky horses. The Appaloosa will always have this type of eye as a natural breed characteristic, and will show it just as prominently when he is calmly grazing in a field as when he is alarmed. It is one of the major identifying points of the breed.

Typical Appaloosa Coat Patterns

Recognized by Appaloosa Horse Club
MOSCOW, IDAHO

Black, white with black spots over loin and hips.

White, black spots over entire body.

Black, white over loin and hips.

Black, white spots over entire body.

Blue roan.

Black, white spots over loin and hips.

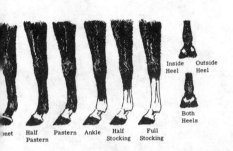

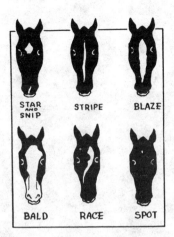

The parts of the horse where the skin is thin, such as around the nostrils or eyes, show another trait in the Appaloosa which is characteristic of the breed and is required for registration of the animal. In these thin-skin areas, there will occur a pink, white and black mottling effect which is known as "parti-colored skin." Although this condition is more prominent in some individuals than in others, it must be present in at least one of three areas on a true Appaloosa: the eyes, the nostrils and mouth, or the genital region.

The basic conformation of the Appaloosa can vary to some degree, as it does in all breeds of horses, dependent upon the work the horse is called upon to do and the market demands of the area in which he is being used. If the Appaloosa is to be used as a working cattle and ranch horse, he will tend to be more muscular in his rear quarters, gaskins and shoulders. If his owner plans a racing or gaming career for him, he will show a leggier appearance, be lighter of body than the cow horse but with well-developed muscles fore and hind, and have the ability and desire to run. As a trail or pleasure horse, the Appaloosa will probably come closest to the basic conformation as defined by the national registry, with characteristics of personality, docility and dependability as the points of primary consideration.

Two of the requirements for Appaloosa registration—white sclera in eye, and parti-colored (mottled) skin—are exhibited by this young Appaloosa mare.

Due to the recent rise in popularity of the Appaloosa, there are some who would breed animals of questionable quality to their Appaloosa stallion, merely to obtain a loud color pattern on the resulting colt. The market's demands for Appaloosas exceeds the current supply and it is often tempting to the less scrupulous horseman to cut into that market by breeding spots onto any horse, regardless of breed (or lack of breed), as long as its owner will pay the breeding fee asked. Eventually, the selectivity of the buying public will greatly reduce or even eliminate the market for animals resulting from such matings, but as long as these kinds of stallion owners are around, they cause confusion and do untold harm to the breed.

A typical "laminated" or striped hoof of the Appaloosa.

It is only natural that a person cherish his or her first horse, regardless of its hazy pedigree and rather apparent faults. A large headed, Roman-nosed, sway-backed, rafter-hipped, crooked-legged, platter-footed equine might mean true beauty and love to the little girl who owns him. And you can be fairly sure his coat will shine with twice the brushings that the most expensive and pampered race or show horse would receive. If this little girl happens to own a mare and gets the "fever" for an Appaloosa colt as well, she presents a real problem to the owner of the Appaloosa stallion whom she may approach to arrange for the breeding. It is very difficult to say "No" to a girl whose love, pride and hope shine so obviously from her face. But if he is to remain true to the standards and ethics of the horse world, he must refuse to accept such a mare for his stallion as gently as possible.

This is not to say that the world should be made up only of highly-bred, registered horses, and that those of poor conformation and questionable parentage should be automatically destroyed. In the first place, there has *never* been a horse which was completely free from faults. *All* have some faults somewhere. The ones with the least command the best price; it's just that simple.

But the horse described earlier that had an over-sized head, big feet and a poorly-made body can provide a young rider with many hours of fun and companionship at a relatively inexpensive cost. He has a definite place in the world of horses, and thousands of horsemen and women received their first lessons from this kind of horse. The point is, however, that neither this horse nor any of its offspring can be properly called an "Appaloosa," regardless of any spotted blanket that may be in evidence. A true Appaloosa will not vary in extreme from the basic conformation set forth in the official Judging Guide, and while outcrosses that carry Appaloosa markings do exist, they cannot be correctly called "Appaloosas" on the basis of their color patterns alone.

Due to the fact that the Appaloosa was almost lost as a breed, a drastic breeding program became necessary to save it from complete extinction. Of the animals which existed at the time Mr. Thompson began to register these horses, few true representatives of the original breed were to be found. Many of the domesticated Appaloosas were used for heavy farm work and showed the result of outcrossing with this type of stock in their ancestry. The Appaloosa's qualities of refinement, necessary in a good saddle horse and noted in the Appaloosas of the Nez Perce by Lewis and Clark, had been lost in many cases through poor breeding programs. The wild stock had crossed with mustangs, paints, and others, making many of them unfit as Foundation Stock for the breed. So, in order to return the breed to its original form in the shortest period of time, Appaloosa breeders were allowed to outcross to other selected breeds and have the resulting foals eligible for registry in the Foundation Stock. Appaloosas with unknown parentage and/or ancestry but which showed true Appaloosa characteristics were eligible for registration in the Tentative Registry.

Today, the Foundation Registry is closed to all additions. The Permanent Registry and the Tentative Registry remain open to horses which meet the requirements, and both have Breeding Stock provisions. A more detailed description of the types of registry and requirements for registration appears in another chapter.

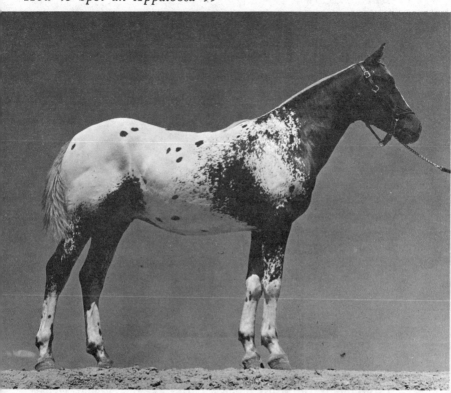

Typical Appaloosa conformation and coat pattern.

The much-discussed color patterns of the Appaloosa come in several varieties and use every base coat color found in other breeds of horses. The markings that are probably most easily recognizable by the average person are those which consist of a white "blanket" over the rear quarters of the animal, in which symmetrical spots of oval, round or elliptical shape are scattered. The base coat may be black, brown, bay or dun, or it may be a combination of any of these colors with a mixture of white hairs, giving either a roan or a mottled appearance. Sometimes the white blanket is only a light, frosty patch with the darker spots almost blending into the darker coat; sometimes it is a bright, well-defined blanket which covers most of the rear quarters and barrel of the animal, and which might stretch all the way to the withers in front.

A second type of pattern is the pure white blanket, such as was

Example of the white blanket pattern of the Appaloosa.

described in the first example, which covers most of the rump, but without any spots appearing in the blanket itself. A variation of this type is a less-defined blanket with the white appearing over the hips more as a light frost. These markings can be found with any base coat color, or be carried on a horse with a roan or mottled front quarter.

A third example of Appaloosa markings is a solid-colored or a roan horse of any normal color, covered with small white spots about the size of a quarter over most of the head and body. No large area of white, such as a blanket, is present with this type of "snowflake" marking.

The fourth type of color pattern is a basic coat color, such as bay or black, with just a light sprinkling of white flecks appearing over the loin and hip region. These flecks and spots are scattered, not solid like a "blanket," and are more in the nature of a patchy or frosty white sprinkling.

A young Appaloosa mare shows the "snowflake" type of coat pattern.

The fifth example is the roan, either "red" or "blue," with the loin and hips showing a lightening of white or frosting. Many individuals carrying this type of marking have a darker concentration of base color over the frontal bones of the head and the hip joints and stifles. These Appaloosas appear to be mottled over most of their bodies, with just a lighter mottling amounting to a slight frosty appearance over the rear quarters. This type of marking is often called a "marble" Appaloosa.

The sixth and last type of color pattern to be listed here is called the "leopard" marking and is described as a white base color with black, sorrel, chestnut or bay spots scattered over the entire body from the head to the hind quarters. Some of these horses will be entirely or almost entirely white in front, but will have the characteristic "raindrop" leopard markings over the loin and hips. The leopard Appaloosa makes a very striking appearance and was often the favorite of royalty for carriage or saddle horses centuries ago. With the blanket-type of pattern, it is one of the two Appaloosa markings most easily recognized from a distance.

These six color patterns can be varied within themselves or can

Young Appaloosa colt with a bright leopard coat pattern.

Leopard markings behind and near-solid color in front give this stallion an unsual appearance, even for an Appaloosa. Notice the regularity of the round and oval-shaped spots. (Midway photo)

be combined together to give even a wider assortment of patterns. The patterns of each Appaloosa is as distinct as a fingerprint, with no two ever having been found exactly alike. It is important to remember that the characteristic coat pattern must be accompanied by the other Appaloosa traits; and above all, these must be found on a horse that meets the conformation standards of the breed.

It is interesting to note that the markings of an Appaloosa are symmetrical and do not give a jagged or ragged appearance. They are not the "blotchy" type often found in pintos, nor are they large, irregular markings as is common in paints and pintos. The spots of an Appaloosa are clearly defined and regular in shape, being comparatively small, usually no bigger than a silver dollar.

When two distinct colors meet on the neck of an Appaloosa, the mane hairs will not change color at the dividing line. In the pinto, the mane hair will be white where the neck is white, and then change to bay where that color makes a pattern on the animal's neck. The mane and tail of an Appaloosa are often made up of a mixture of black and white or brown and white hairs, giving an appearance of a person who is just beginning to turn grey.

With many members of the animal and bird kingdoms the male of the species is the most colorfully marked; and this seems to hold true of the Appaloosa as well. While there are exceptions, it is common to find the most loudly marked color pattern on the male Appaloosa, and the marble or mottled pattern more often on the mares. Of course, there are many brightly colored and beautifully marked mares, and a number of rather drab colored stallions and geldings, to provide the exceptions which prove the general rule.

Some people will confuse a certain type of roan common to horses carrying Tennessee Walker blood, with Appaloosa markings. These roan horses will have white coming up from the belly and rear legs, have a wide blaze on their faces, and show white about the jowls. They often have mottled skin around their noses and eyes, and some even will show a white sclera encircling the eye. The markings found on these types of roans are not the same shape and placings as those on an Appaloosa, and they are further characterized by having full manes and tails, while the Appaloosa's mane and tail are sparse. A so-called "flea-bitten grey" horse is sometimes confused with the Appaloosa, as are other coat markings carried by Pintos and horses that show dark spots which are common in bays, browns, sorrels and chestnuts of nearly every breed.

Sometimes, through an ill-advised mating, a horse is born showing definite and true Appaloosa characteristics such as a blanket with spots over the hips, parti-colored skin around the nose and eyes, the white sclera in the eye, and striped hooves, but all in combination with other markings which are characteristic of the Pinto, or with conformation showing signs of pony, draft or Albino ancestry. Horses having draft, pony, paint, Pinto or Albino breeding, or showing evidence of the roan described previously, are not eligible for registration as an Appaloosa. Furthermore, matings between registered Appaloosas and these horses and ponies are frowned upon and actively discouraged by the National Registry, even when the owner of the resulting foal makes no attempt to apply for registration.

Boots, socks and stockings often appear on the feet and legs of the Appaloosa, and add a great deal to their flashy appearance. A high stocking that reaches the knee or hock, however, is not permissible since this is an indication of Pinto breeding. A common marking on the legs of the Appaloosa is the so-called "flash" marking, which is an elongated splash of white that appears on the lower portion of the leg. Sometimes several of these will be present on one or more leg of the Appaloosa and are quite colorful.

One of the interesting things about raising a young Appaloosa colt or filly is that he or she may often change coat pattern throughout the first five years of life. Many Appaloosa colts are born as "solids," showing no characteristic coat pattern at all, but having the white sclera, parti-colored skin and, of course, the basic Appaloosa conformation. Until the colt shows definite color pattern markings, he is eligible for registration as "Breeding Stock" in either the Tentative or the Permanent Registry, according to the status of registration of his sire and dam. This means that, while he is fully registered in every other respect, he is not eligible for show or exhibition until such time as his coat pattern develops sufficiently to become easily recognizable.

A new foal is quite often born with one Appaloosa color pattern, changing to a completely different pattern as he or she grows older. This condition is somewhat more common with the fillies than the male colts. Many good mares are born with little or no color pattern apparent, and then develop more roaning and mottling each spring as their winter hair sheds, until at maturity they show a strong, recognizable pattern. It is not uncommon for a colt to be born with a well-defined spotted blanket on his rear, and to have this pattern gradually change into a leopard type by the time he reaches one or two years of age.

Two major factors influence many of the changes that occur in color patterns of Appaloosas: the dilution factor, and the greying gene. The first of these is merely a condition where very little contrast exists between the base coat color and the white markings. It is common in crosses between an Appaloosa and a dun or Palomino. It is often nearly impossible to detect the white markings of the Appaloosa on a horse with a light, creamy-colored base coat, and is a cross that is highly discouraged by the National Registry.

The greying gene is an even more serious problem. Hereditary

A young colt and filly out of the same dam. Notice how their patterns are changing from blanket types to leopards as they lose the darker body hair.

traits of all animals are transmitted by the parents through the genes. In horses, the greying gene is carried in addition to the usual genes for color, and causes dark hairs to be replaced by white hairs in a very short time after the birth of a foal. This greying factor has been put into the genes by a cross breeding to a grey horse somewhere in the foal's ancestry, and once added into the genetic make-up of that bloodline, it will rob generation after succeeding generation of Appaloosas of their characteristic color patterns.

The typical newborn foal carrying this greying gene will greet life with prominent Appaloosa coat markings; but by weaning time the spots and dark-colored hairs will fade due to a large percentage of white hairs which will have started to appear. By the time the foal is a year old, the colored areas will have become grey and his once-dark spots will hardly be discernible. When he reaches two years, or at the most three years of age, he will be a very light grey or white horse with no Appaloosa markings apparent in his coat at all.

The result of the greying gene's presence should not be confused with the natural "roaning" that commonly takes place with Appaloosas as they grow older. Many Appaloosas are born a solid color, but gradually turn to a "red" or "blue" roan as white hairs mix with the darker color of the base coat over a prolonged period of time. In these cases, the spots of the Appaloosa do not lose their original depth of color, and the roaning process affects only the base coat, particularly in the forequarters. On the other hand, the effects of the greying gene result in bleaching out *all* color from the horse, including spots; and this loss of color is very rapid.

Genetics of the Appaloosa color patterns are currently being studied closely to determine what system, if any, can be detected to help future breeding programs to produce a more uniform number of well colored foals. Professor R. W. Miller of Montana State College is making a study of this subject for his doctoral thesis at the time of this writing. Material collected and tabulated from the files of the Appaloosa Horse Club, Inc. in Moscow, Idaho, is being sorted by computer and will eventually be analyzed by similar electronic equipment; the results will be published and made available to Appaloosa owners. Until scientific data becomes public, however, the color pattern factor in Appaloosa breeding remains an interesting and intriguing gamble.

It is not uncommon for two Appaloosa parents having predominately bay-and-white markings to produce a black-and-white colt. There are also a number of cases recorded where an Appaloosa mare or stallion will consistently produce or sire solid-colored foals when mated to an Appaloosa, but will just as consistently turn out highly colored foals when bred to a solid colored animal with no known Appaloosa background. Such contradictions only add to the fun of raising Appaloosas.

A poll taken from a wide number of Appaloosa owners in recent years has shown that there seems to be no preference of one color pattern over any of the others. While some individuals favor one type, this is balanced by the likes and dislikes of someone else. Because the greatest emphasis is placed on conformation and its approach to the optimum standard, the type of color pattern becomes secondary in importance to most reputable breeders. This is not to deny, however, that a good color pattern on a good Appaloosa is the ultimate goal of everyone who awaits the arrival of a new Appaloosa foal. That additional excitement generated by the anticipation of the color pattern is one of the main reasons Appaloosa breeders are so enthusiastic.

Almost every type of Appaloosa color pattern can be seen at this Riverside, California show. (Photo by Miehle Studios)

Summing it all up, the Appaloosa can be defined as a good saddle horse which carries one of the characteristic color patterns of the breed and shows white sclera in the eye and a pink-and-black mottling around his eyes, nostrils, lips and/or genital parts. He must have a high, well-defined wither; and because of both his basic structure and his inheritance, should prove himself to be a top-notch rough country horse. He is sure-footed and rarely has foot or leg troubles. His disposition is one of docility and intelligence, but somewhat independent. He is a dependable mount, and therefore an excellent choice for anyone—be he an inexperienced child, a working cowboy, or a show rider.

While the Appaloosa shows quality and refinement throughout, he's tough and will give his rider a full day's work. The ability of the Appaloosa to withstand the rigors of long races and difficult hunts was one of the main reasons he was so desired by the Indian warrior, and this ability is very much in evidence in the breed today. Perhaps a phrase quoted from a hard-working cowpuncher sums it up best. He had ridden and worked with just about every type of stock horse we have around, and when asked how he liked the Appaloosa, his answer echoed the appreciation every horseman feels after a long ride on a good horse: "You can sure tell the difference when you come in at night."

3
Buying An Appaloosa

The selection of a horse is an important decision that will affect your bank account, your disposition, and your future way of life—hopefully in a pleasant and enjoyable way. But a happy choice will rarely be achieved by accident; it must be based on careful, unemotional consideration of many things. The novice may want to enlist the aid of a horseman in whose knowledge he has respect and confidence. If he is a good horseman, he can help to make a wise selection. If he is not qualified, he could steer you into a bad choice, and you'd be better off without him.

The selection of expert help can become almost as difficult as the selection of the horse itself. No one would think of calling himself an expert surgeon or expert bricklayer without having had many years of serious study and experience in these fields, and it takes no less knowledge and skill to make an expert horseman. Yet for some reason, there seem almost to be more "experts" in the horse world than there are horses! Owning a horse, or even being around horses all one's life, does not make an expert horseman, anymore than taking a lot of airplane rides makes one a pilot or navigator. Too many so-called "expert" horsemen are "practical" men who have done a lot of riding, but most of it the wrong way. They exhibit scorn for anyone who studies horses from books, without ever realizing the importance of scientific and theoretical knowledge to the truly expert horse trainer and horse breeder.

Everyone who owns a horse should attempt to learn as much as possible about horses. This means a lot of hours spent in reading as well as riding. If this knowledge can be obtained before purchasing, the buyer has a better basis upon which to make his selection. If not, it becomes necessary to rely on the knowledge and advice of someone in whom he can place his confidence. The person who has gained the respect of many other horsemen is usually a pretty good bet.

In the selection of a horse, one must first decide the use or uses to which this particular horse is going to be put. Is he to be a family mount? Will he be used by just one, or by all members of the family? Will he be used as a breeding animal? Will he be shown, either in halter classes or performance, or perhaps in games and races? Will he need to be extensively trained, or is he to be primarily used as a weekend pleasure and trail riding horse? The answers to these and other questions will have a great deal to do with the proper selection of a horse by a potential buyer.

The family pet can be just a good grade of saddle horse of about any breed or combination of breeds; or he can be a purebred. The major considerations in such a decision should revolve around: (1) the animal's disposition, (2) the price one can afford to pay, and (3) the amount and type of training that the horse will need for the purposes he will be used for.

If the horse is to be used more as a pet than anything else, especially if in a family where there are small children, it is very important that an animal with a gentle, docile nature be selected. Often called a "kid's horse," his age is not of very much importance, so long as he isn't too young. Many good horses of twelve years and beyond can provide eight to ten additional years of pleasure for some family. But his disposition must be cooperative and pleasing, and not grouchy or flighty.

Prices will vary with geography, season of the year, and merits of the individual horse. A young, unbroke colt would probably cost less than a trained, mature animal; but the expense of feeding and caring for this colt until he is old enough to ride, and the eventual cost of breaking and training him, make the bargain questionable. The novice should beware of buying any horse that is wild or unbroken, especially those that have been running free in a large pasture or field without benefit of much handling or training. The initial cost of these animals may be less than the prices of trained horses which are well broken to saddle, but the risk of serious injury is ever present and very probable whenever unbroke horses are being handled. A few additional dollars on the purchase price will buy a horse dependably trained to give his owner a lifetime of enjoyment; and they will be dollars well spent.

Generally speaking, one could expect to pay a minimum of $200–$400 for a registered Appaloosa gelding of some merit and broken to ride. For this money, one cannot expect an outstanding pedigree of famous bloodlines, or a top winner in the shows, or a fancy spotted blanket, or a finished stock or cutting horse. But the buyer *can* expect the animal to be sound and healthy, of respectable quality, to have a good-natured disposition, to be in good condition, to have his registration papers in order, and to have any inclinations to buck or bolt well removed from his mind. If a breeding animal or top winner of halter or performance classes at shows is desired, the price will very quickly climb into several thousands of dollars, especially if any specific training has been given to him.

Because horse training requires a great deal of skill and knowledge and is time-consuming if it is to be effective, it is understandably costly. A green-broke horse can easily double or triple his original value after he has spent several months with a good trainer. This kind of expense is usually only justified when the owner plans an ambitious show career for the horse, or when he needs the horse trained for some specific job. A pleasure horse rarely requires this much professional work. Breaking the horse to saddle, however, should be done by an expert—a *real* one, not just a self-styled "expert." A good horse can be ruined in short order by improper breaking and training methods, and care should be taken in the selection of the man to break any horse to saddle.

The best choice for a family horse is always a gelding; a mare is a fair second choice. A stallion is *never* a good selection for anyone except the person who is in the horse breeding business. Appaloosa stallions are about as easy to handle as any stallion

Typical Appaloosa gelding that makes a good all-around using horse.

will ever be, but regardless of how gentle an individual animal may ordinarily be, a stallion will always present the possibility of serious danger to his owner and rider and others who might be handling horses nearby, especially during the breeding season. Since this season occurs at the same time of year that most people have the opportunity to ride—the summertime—this danger is increased. A young person should never be allowed to handle a stallion unless he or she is well trained and experienced, and only then under certain supervised conditions. A stallion is a breeding animal, and only recognized breeders and experienced trainers have the knowledge and skill required to properly handle stallions. They are certainly no choice for a family horse.

While a mare makes a good family mount, her owner will almost always yield to a horseman's natural desire to raise a colt, and she'll eventually be converted into a brood mare. Although a bred mare can and often should be ridden throughout her pregnancy, she still loses a great deal as a good, all-around saddle horse under these conditions. She will often shows signs of crankiness during her 11-month gestation period, and as time goes on, she just isn't going to have the pep and spirit she once had. After the colt is born, there is always the problem of having the colt run alongside his mother when you want to take a ride. So, unless the mare will be spayed, thereby insuring her removal from the brood mare classification, she is only a fair choice as a family horse.

This brings us right back to the gelding, the preference of the cowboy and working stockman, required as a cavalry horse by the Army, and unquestionably the best choice for general use of any kind. Usually of gentle and tractable nature, the gelding presents no breeding-season problems; he is ready to go whenever his owner wants to use him. Price-wise, a gelding is often more reasonably priced than a breeding animal; but a good, trained gelding will always command a better market price than a second- or third-rate stallion.

Physical condition of the horse is a matter of prime importance to a buyer. A sick or unsound horse is never a bargain. A reputable breeder will give the buyer an honest appraisal of the animals he is offering for sale, and will never attempt to "palm off" a sick or lame horse on an unsuspecting customer. Unfortunately, the largest number of horses for sale are handled by horse traders, not breeders or breeding farms, and here is where the buyer had better be extremely wary; for even the most experienced horsemen are often victims at the hands of clever, unscrupulous men. There are, of course, a number of honest and ethical horse dealers, but every community also has their share of the disreputable traders whose ilk have been cheating the public on horse sales since time immemorial. Typically, this man boasts of a lifetime of knowledge about horses and freely disseminates information (largely exaggerated) to potential buyers. His manner is one of complete authority and his major stock in trade is a glib tongue and a corral full of sorry beasts that are too handicapped by injury and disease to be of much value to anyone. Sometimes he has what appears to be an excellent horse for sale. This one will have a long story, a high price, and some bad faults you won't detect until he's home and he's yours.

The dishonest horse trader does more than overcharge the buyer; he frequently sells horses that will cost the new owner many more dollars in vet and feed bills, and worse, might be of such a nature that the rider could be seriously injured by the animal. In short, when buying a horse, do not be misled by advertising, written or verbal. Avoid all but the dealers and breeders who have reputations for treating their customers honestly and fairly. If possible, enlist the aid of a good horseman to help you evaluate the horses you see.

Do not be too alarmed if you see minor cuts, scratches, scars or blemishes on a horse. Unless he is a carefully handled show animal, no horse reaches middle age without having picked up some of these along the way. Be sure, however, that the marks stem from *minor* injuries and are not major causes of eventual lameness, or indications of a bad hereditary condition. A horse that shows signs of lameness or disease will be the most expensive bargain you ever made!

It costs just as much to feed a poor horse as a good one; in fact, the horse with bad teeth or a malformed jaw, or one that has digestive troubles or is infested with external or internal parasites, will cost his owner much *more* for feed, and will still look like a poor horse. In addition, higher and more frequent vet bills are almost always the case with such an animal, and he rarely provides his rider with satisfactory service.

As you can see, there are a number of factors to consider when making the selection of a horse besides the initial cost. As most horsemen will tell you, the initial cost of the animal is usually the least amount, percentage-wise, of your total investment in a horse.

Summing it up, the best choice is probably a mature gelding which is sound and free from disease. He must have a dependable and docile disposition, be well broken to saddle, and fairly "kid-proof," yet contain enough spirit to provide a good ride. He should have an appearance in which his owner can take some pride, and he must be priced somewhere close to his actual value. You can find a horse like this in just about any breed, or even in a "combination-of-breeds" animal; but if you want to diminish the gamble, you'll start by looking for an Appaloosa.

Few breeds offer the disposition and versatility found in an Appaloosa horse. He will carry Dad in a fast, exciting race, and

The disposition of the Appaloosa makes him an ideal family horse, as this young family will agree.

immediately be calm enough to allow the youngsters to climb aboard bareback. He'll give Mom a good, sunny day ride without a lot of foolish spooking, and he's easy to catch and handle in the home pasture. All this, and a flashy polka-dotted hide besides. And he can be found in just about any price range!

There are several specific things to keep in mind regarding the purchase of an Appaloosa besides the general considerations that go with the purchase of any horse. While the bright coat of the Appaloosa is one of his most appealing features, it can have a definite adverse effect on the pocketbook of the buyer. In other words, the louder the color, the higher the price. There's really nothing wrong with this system, as long as the horse under that bright color is a good one. But all too often, and especially with the horse trader, Appaloosa with highly marked colored coat patterns are priced far too high for their actual value, because too many buyers can be found that don't look beyond the color. The prime and most important factor in buying a horse is to remember to first look for a healthy and sound animal, and one with a dependable and obedient nature. Everything else is a bonus.

Since a gelding should be first choice for the family, it should be pointed out that there are relatively few Appaloosa geldings that carry an extremely colorful coat pattern. It is a common practice among breeders to alter any male horse which does not have a particularly colorful coat, unless he is just too outstanding conformation-wise to eliminate as a breeding animal. When a highly colored Appaloosa is gelded, it might mean that his owner just wanted a brightly colored riding or show horse of outstanding quality; or, it could mean that the animal carried too many faults to be allowed use as a breeding stallion. When you see an Appaloosa gelding with a dazzling color pattern, look first at his general conformation. If it is good and sound and healthy, and he's for sale, you'd better start reaching for that old wallet! When buying, always make the quality of the horse the first consideration, and color a secondary matter. And don't be disappointed if you find everything you want in an Appaloosa except a big white blanket with dollar-sized spots. He'll still give you Appaloosa performance and disposition, and for that, he's worth a great deal. Both Buffalo Bill and Chief Joseph used Appaloosas, and their favorite mounts were rather drab-colored geldings.

Perhaps the horse that's being sought is intended for a more specialized purpose than a general family horse; for example, perhaps only one member of the family is going to use and ride him. The growing popularity of horses among young people, especially girls, has been continually on the increase ever since the end of World War II; and horses owned by youth comprise the largest segment of the nation's horse population. As a rule, the boy or girl who owns a horse rarely has much of a choice of places where he or she can ride. While some Westerners are still fortunate enough to live where they can take their horse out from the home pasture for a day's ride without encountering fences, plowed fields, highways or housing developments, the number is very small. For the most part, it is necessary to confine the riding to the pasture, a riding academy arena, or a saddle club's ring. Such limitations are frustrating, and many who are unable to have trails available on which to ride find their pleasure horseback riding in the show ring.

Basically, there are three types of show classes for the horseman. The breeding or halter class requires the least amount of training but is almost always open only to registered horses. The performance classes encompass a wide variety of events that require the horse to be shown under saddle or in harness (for some breeds). For Appaloosas, the Western Pleasure, English Pleasure, Indian Costume, Stock Horse and Trail Horse classes are among the most popular. These require a lot of training, but much of this can be done by an owner-rider with desire, ability and a good horse. Some of these classes are "open," which means the horses in them can be registered or not; in other shows, the same classes might be closed to any horse excepting those which are registered. In breed shows, such as all-Appaloosa shows, only registered horses are allowed to participate in any of the events.

Shows which offer competitive games on horseback or gymkhana events usually have them open to all breeds or combination of breeds; but in breed shows, of course, these would be restricted to horses of that breed.

The choice of a horse for a young boy or girl should rest on certain additional considerations. If the rider is going to be using the horse only in neighborhood competition or in the company of the neighbors or in a limited number of small local horse shows, a registered animal commanding a higher price may not be justified. Even if he or she intends to use the horse in competitive games such as pole bending or barrel racing, it is still possible to attend a lot of shows and not need a registered horse in order to participate. If, however, the interest lies toward larger regional or national shows, or if there is any plan to breed horses, then a registered animal is the only logical choice.

Once Dad has agreed to buy a horse, he'd better resign himself to spending the next sunny weekend devoted to the search, as everyone who has ever truly wanted to own a horse will understand. If the family lives in a small or even medium-sized town, the problem of locating horse farms and dealers in the vicinity is a simple matter of a few inquiries. But if their home is in or near a large city, the problem of locating a suitable horse may be a major one. The classified ad section of the newspaper offers the obvious solution, but it has serious drawbacks. Many of the ads are placed by horse traders who have overrated horses for sale; a few are placed by people who are moving or otherwise need to sell a good horse; and a very small minority are placed by the most desirable source of horses for sale, the breeding farm. If more breeders would do more "institutional" advertising so that potential buyers and visiting horsemen could more easily locate their farms, it couldn't help but favorably affect their overall sales, and it would certainly be a service to novice and experienced buyers alike.

If it is decided that a registered horse is to be the choice, then a short request to the breed registry office will bring quick assistance in the form of names and addresses of local breeders, or of someone locally who can help with the problem. The Appaloosa Horse Club in Moscow, Idaho, is always efficient and cooperative in providing free information and aid. Sometimes a member of a regional affiliate of the association can give directions and information about horses for sale and location of breeding farms

The beginning of a good friendship.

in the area. Taking the precaution of inquiring first from an official source may very well save dollars and headaches later.

One should never be afraid of being "obligated" when visiting a reputable breeder. Most Appaloosa breeders are very friendly and helpful, and honestly enjoy answering questions and "talking horse" with their visitors. Even though you may not make a choice on your first visit, you should not feel backward about asking to see and even to ride animals that interest you. Only the man with something to hide is reluctant to show you his stock of horses. Most breeders take pleasure and pride in being given the opportunity to exhibit their animals to you.

When buying a registered horse, be cautious about accepting statements or promises about the registration status of the animal, especially when buying from someone other than an established breeder. If you are shown registration papers or a certificate, examine it carefully to make sure it is in order. Do not accept any verbal assurances that the horse is eligible for registration, or that his papers will be sent to you as soon as they are received from the breed registry offices. When a man has a horse for sale, everything about that horse should be in order before a buyer sees him. If he's eligible for registration, then the horse should be completely registered, his Registration Certificate in order and available for inspection, before he is offered for sale—especially if the seller is trying to get registered horse prices. Far too many buyers have learned too late that their newly purchased horse is not as he was represented by the seller, particularly insofar as his eligibility for registration is concerned. Play it safe; before any money passes hands, make absolutely certain that the horse is actually and properly registered with the Appaloosa Horse Club and that the Registration Certificate is received at the same time you take delivery on the animal.

The benefits received in owning an Appaloosa horse are far greater than would fit in any bank. The hours of pleasure and enjoyment so derived will increase with the amount of time horse and owner spend together. But we live in a practical world, and this new relationship is always more firmly founded when it begins with the buyer getting a good value for his money. These pointers should help you get started in the right direction; your Appaloosa will do the rest!

4
Facts About Breeding

Few sights give more pleasure than watching a sassy Appaloosa colt, running and kicking up his young heels on a warm, sunny day. Few moments of anticipation are more keenly felt than the moments spent by the owner of a cherished Appaloosa mare before she gives birth to her long-awaited foal. And few Appaloosa owners can truthfully deny that they haven't met an overwhelming desire to raise a spotted colt or two at some time during their Appaloosa-owning career. The person who owns a gelding is usually fairly successful in remembering that breeding of horses is best left to the professional horse breeder, and he can more or less content himself with the vicarious pleasure of watching a colt from a distance. But the person who owns a mare quite often yields to the inevitable, and sooner or later starts searching for the stallion to sire the sure-to-be-a-prize-winning colt from his mare.

The search for such a stallion should be a lot more than a casual inspection of the neighborhood pastures. Even those who live close to a good Appaloosa breeding farm may not locate the right stallion for their mare here, unless a number of different stallions are avalable. The business of genetics is a very involved science, and a good colt is not an accident; he is the result of planned and careful mating of a good horse to a good mare. A breeding of

54

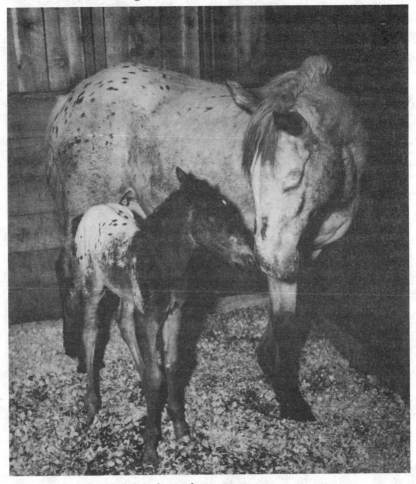

A tender moment.

any less consideration does a serious injustice to the horse industry, and will almost always produce a colt that is, at best, mediocre. Since the population of mediocre-to-poor horses is already far too high, it would hardly be fair to contribute another colt to it, just to satisfy your desire for one.

Assuming your mare is a good individual with respectable bloodlines behind her, then her colt could reasonably be expected to be a credit to his breed and his owner. But it takes more than just a good, registered Appaloosa stallion for the sire of this colt; it requires careful matching of the individual characteristics and pedigrees of both stallion and mare before one can be hopeful of a good colt. If the mare tends to be rather long in her back, a short-coupled stallion should be sought. Every fault, insofar as possible, should be compensated for. The genes won't always combine the way you hope and plan they will, but your chances are far better with this kind of planning than without.

Naturally, since you're breeding Appaloosas, you want to select a sire that has shown proven ability to throw well-colored colts. All stallions have a certain percentage of "solid" colts born every year. Some of these color out before they reach maturity; some never do. A stallion with a high percentage of colored colts to his credit is a better risk. To be sure, check his record at the office of the Appaloosa Horse Club, Inc.

If you are able to locate a satisfactory stallion close to home, you are fortunate. If, however, the best match means you must transport the mare a reasonable distance, the time and expense involved in doing so is well spent. Do not yield to the temptation of just using the best of what's handy. Most people are unable to afford both the time and money needed to take the mare to a stallion 3,000 miles away, regardless of how choice the match would be. But there are many which are closer that are excellent potential sires for your colt, if you will spend the time and care to find them.

The time to study the available stallions' records and pedigrees is during the winter, not when spring's arrival makes it important to get the mare bred at the earliest possible time. If done a sufficient time in advance, it is possible to write to various stallion owners and gather important facts regarding the stallion's record as a sire, performance horse, etc. Advance arrangements with the breeder are much better than last-minute inquiries, and prevent disappointment if you should find the stallion's book is full early in the season, as it often is for the top horses.

It is generally a good idea to arrange to bring the mare to the breeding farm a day or so ahead of her breeding period. This will allow her time to settle down and become accustomed to her new surroundings, and may make the difference between her becoming safely in foal and not.

Prize mares and geldings on the old Pete French ranch, a famous early-day spread in southeastern Oregon. (Henry Sheldon photo)

Most breeding farms and stallion owners who have facilities to take care of visiting mares will charge a nominal fee of $1.00 or $1.50 per day for the mare's care and feed while she is on their place. If she is a young mare or has a history of being hard to "settle," or if she's been transported for quite a distance, it is wise to consider leaving her at the breeding farm for the twenty-one days until her next heat to allow the stallion owner to check her. If she is found to be still "open" (not pregnant), the repeat breeding will present fewer problems. This is precautionary, of course, but it would eliminate having to haul her back and forth between your home and the stallion if you should find, later in the season, that she has not settled to the stallion's service.

Most stallion owners allow "return in season" which means the mare may be returned for service at no additional breeding fee if this is done prior to a published date, such as December 31 of the current year. With some breeders, the date is earlier. By not returning in season, you lose the stud fee you paid, plus a productive year for the mare. The best way to avoid these troubles is just to stand the $25–$40 additional expense in leaving the mare an extra three weeks at the breeding farm.

Some stallion owners require a booking fee, or advance fee, to "reserve" a breeding from their stallion for the current or approaching season. Some of the more popular stallions might be booked ahead a year or more. The booking fee varies, but generally runs about 25 per cent of the total stud fee. The balance, or the entire breeding fee if no advance has been paid, is paid at the time the mare leaves the breeding farm. Rarely is there such a thing as credit insofar as breeding and boarding fees are concerned, and one should be prepared to make full payment before arrangements are made.

It is always a good idea to have a thorough understanding, preferably in writing, with the stallion owner as to what guaran-

APPALOOSA HORSE CLUB BREEDING CERTIFICATE STUB
For Stallion Owners Records

Stallion .... No. ....

Mare .... No. ....

Date of Breeding ....

....

(Or from .... to ....)

Mare Owner ....

Address ....

Remarks ....

The stallion owner agrees to file the annual stallion report with the Appaloosa Horse Club, Inc.

APPALOOSA HORSE CLUB, INC.
MOSCOW, IDAHO
BREEDING CERTIFICATE

This Breeding Certificate must accompany the resulting foal's Application for Registration.

I hereby certify that my stallion .... No. ....

served the mare .... No. .... on the .... day of

........................., 19........, or if pasture bred, was exposed from the ....day of ....,

19........, until the .... day of ...., 19....... .

The above mare does not show any evidence of Pony, Draft, Pinto or Albino breeding. It is not the type of roan pictured in figures 9 to 25 of the pamphlet "Appaloosa Color Patterns, Characteristics and Descriptions."

Signed ....   Signed ....
    Name and address of owner of mare at time of service   Name of stallion owner at time of service

Address ....   Address ....

The stallion owner agrees to file the annual stallion report with the Appaloosa Horse Club, Inc.

Facsimile Breeding Certificate.

tees are promised, what is meant by "in season," etc. This should be done before any breeding arrangements are made. Many stallion owners will have a printed agreement form which completely outlines their obligations and those of the mare owner. Both of you will be required to read and sign this document, and copies are provided for each of you. Such a written agreement eliminates many misunderstandings that might occur later.

The owner of the stallion, or his agent, should give you a signed breeder's certificate, showing the exact dates your mare was served and the name and registration number of both stallion and mare. These certificates are provided by the Appaloosa Horse Club, Inc. to all stallion owners and it is *very* important that you insist on having one that is completed and signed given to you at the time you pay the stud and board fees when taking the mare home. When you wish to apply for registration of the colt the following year, you will be denied the registration unless this signed breeding certificate is attached to the application form. Some breeders prefer to mail all completed breeder's certificates together after the season ends. This is done so that any repeat breedings that may have taken place will show on the certificate. If you agree to this system, you should receive your certificate about the first of the year. If you do not receive it in a reasonable length of time, make sure you contact the breeder and get one from him at once. This certificate is part of what you buy when you pay a stallion fee, and it is a very important piece of paper insofar as the registration of the new colt is concerned. If there is the slightest chance that the stallion owner may move or be otherwise difficult to find, insist on receiving the certificate at the time you pay the fee in full.

Breeding fees for Appaloosa stallions vary all the way from $25 to $1,000, with the average running from $100 to $200. The amount of fee which is charged is usually relative to the type and quality of colts the stallion has thrown in the past, the show record of the stallion, the registration status of the stallion (whether Tentative or Permanent Registry), and of course, the individual merits of the stallion himself. Backyard breeders seldom live up to expectations of their patrons, and a $10 breeding fee will usually give you a $10 colt. The recognized breeder is the least expensive and most reliable man to deal with in the long

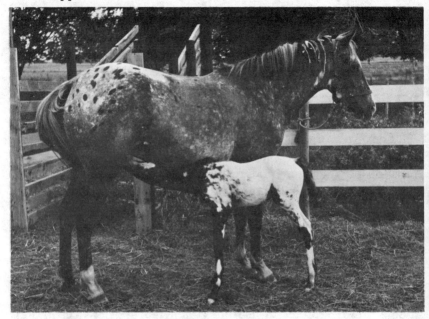

Lunch break.

run. His fee may be a little higher, but he's always in the same place and can be found without difficulty if you have any questions or wish to breed your mare back later. Your mare will be well-fed and cared for, and you won't bring her home from a reputable breeding farm with a runny nose, worms, lice, or any number of other unpleasant things that are present in many of the fly-by-night places.

The respectable breeder takes every precaution to keep his stock, barns and pastures free from disease and parasites, and many of them require a veterinarian's inspection of the mares before they arrive to prevent any possible outbreak of disease. This is for the protection of the other visiting mares as well as the breeder's own animals. No one should ever attempt to take a sick mare to a stallion, or anywhere else except a veterinarian for that matter. In 90 per cent of the cases, a mare that is sick will not settle to service and she'll only create trouble and expense for her owner if an attempt is made to serve her while she is not in good condition.

A field of brood mares that any horseman would be proud to own.

Stallion owners often require that the hind shoes be pulled off the mare, for the protection of the stallion. One should inquire whether this precaution will be required so that the shoes may be taken off before the mare leaves home.

The owner of every registered Appaloosa stallion is required to complete a Stallion Report each year by the Appaloosa Horse Club, Inc. This report contains a list of names, registration numbers, descriptions, etc. of every mare served by that stallion, and the dates of service for each. These are due on January 1 of each year and are very important as far as the owners of the mares are concerned. No applications for registration showing this stallion as sire of the colt will be honored unless the mare is recorded on this annual report. It is, in effect, a certified confirmation by the stallion owner that your mare was actually bred to the horse on specified dates, and by so certifying, he eliminates the possibility of someone trying to list his stallion as the sire of a colt when he actually is not. With an established breeding farm, good records are kept and reports such as this one are efficiently and accurately filed. The backyard breeder rarely keeps any records, usually fails to file the annual Stallion Report as he should, and presents a real problem to both the owner of the mare and the Appaloosa Horse Club, Inc. The headaches saved in this one department alone by dealing with an established breeding farm more than make up for the difference in stud fees.

Once the mare has returned home, she is considered to be in foal. However, this can be definitely established through examination by a qualified veterinarian about forty-five days after her last service, and it is an inexpensive and wise precaution to take. A mare may well show no signs of heat at the expected times and still be "open." If she did not settle, then she should be returned to the stallion at the earliest possible time in order to save the money spent on the breeding, and to insure as early a foaling date for the mare the following year as you can. The gestation period for a mare is roughly eleven months. When you have her bred,

A three-day-old Appaloosa foal is really in clover.

you invest a substantial amount of money, effort, and inconvenience on your part, and almost a full year's time of waiting. The small fee for an examination to set your mind at rest that she is, indeed, safely in foal is just good insurance.

5

Showing the Appaloosa

The horse show provides an exciting and challenging phase to horse ownership that becomes more popular every year. The wide range, from a very formal Madison Square Garden or Pacific International show, to the local saddle club's gymkhana, provides competitive events for every type of horse, rider, ability and pocketbook. There are shows open only to members of certain organizations under whose rules it is run; and shows open only to horses of a specific breed; and shows for registered horses of any breed. Some shows emphasize classes for horses shown under flat saddle; some slant their events toward the Western rider. There are shows made up entirely of games and racing events, and others that list none of these. In short, there are shows and show events for everyone all over the country, making it possible for just about every horse owner to satisfy any desire he might have for this type of competition.

The horse show that offers substantial prize money to the winning horses and/or elaborate trophies will draw most of the professional trainers and riders from the area, making it pretty difficult to bring home a ribbon, although it's been done more than once. Competition in these shows is usually at such a high pitch that much of the enjoyment and fun is removed, and it is not a good environment for a novice horse or a novice showman.

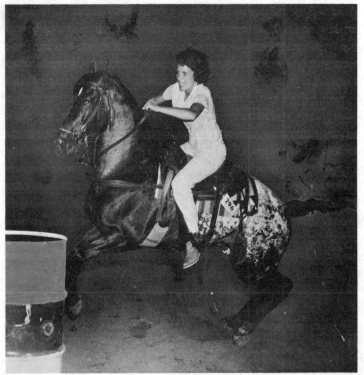

Horse and rider share the excitement of a hotly contested Camas Prairie Stump Race.

By and large, the local horse show or the all-breed show will offer the optimum in challenge–enjoyment ratio to the biggest percentage of horsemen. While professional and semi-professional trainers and riders can often be found at these events, show management will nearly always provide classes for the amateur, making a well-balanced program for exhibitor and spectator alike.

Game events, such as barrel racing or pole-bending, are very popular with young horsemen and women, for several reasons. The requirements in equipment and training are minimal, and the excitement of racing is irresistible. Riders in these events wear blue jeans, boots, a clean shirt and a Western hat (at least at the beginning of the race!). They must have a fast horse which is skillful at turning quickly, and is supple and light. Once the horse is broke to ride, training consists primarily in much practice, and the necessary barrels and poles are inexpensive and easy to set up in a nearby pasture or lot. It is a sport for the young horseman, and the winning horse wins because he runs the course in the least amount of time. This is very important to the spirits of the competitors. All too often in other performance events, the judge's eye is taken by outstanding appointments of horse or rider, and sad as it may seem, the horse giving the best performance may go under a lesser horse whose rider is more versed in the "showmanship" of the show ring. Right or wrong, it is difficult for a proud horse owner to accept. While seeming injustice can always be found where there is competition, there appears to be less chance of finding it in the racing events, which provides the most fun for the most riders at the least cost.

Appaloosa owners take a great deal of pride and pleasure in showing their animals, particularly when competing against all breeds. Here is where the versatility and speed so admired by their Indian owners years ago pays off. Appaloosas are frequently found with winning ribbons in all types of classes such as Western Pleasure, Trail Horse, Stock Horse, Cutting Horse, English pleasure, all games and gymkhana events, and even Hunter and Jumper classes. Lately, there has been a large swing into the flat (or track)

In a Get of Sire class, the sire is not shown; he is represented by three of his offspring and is judged on their quality. The get of the Appaloosa stallion "Chatawa" is being shown here.

racing field, and Appaloosas are proving their worth here as never before.

Another form of horse show most enjoyed by owners of registered Appaloosa horses is the breed show in which only those horses which are registered with the Appaloosa Horse Club, Inc. are allowed to participate. Almost every state holds at least one all-Appaloosa show each year; Texas offers literally dozens. These local or state shows are sponsored and put on by the regional affiliated groups and provide one of the finest opportunities of showing and learning an Appaloosa owner could have. A full selection of halter, performance and racing classes are generally offered, with prizes consisting of ribbons, trophies and (sometimes) money. Whether the horse is a young foal or a fully mature, trained horse, there is a place for him in the show ring.

Nowhere in the show horse world is the novice made to feel so welcome as at the Appaloosa breed show. Being naturally friendly folks to begin with, the more experienced "hands" are always ready with help and advice for the person attending his or her first horse show. It is natural for an amateur to feel somewhat embarrassed and apprehensive, but he soon finds himself with new friends and a lot more confidence. He is made to feel welcome because he *is* welcome, and the experience and pleasure derived here will be invaluable.

The Appaloosa Horse Club, Inc. sponsors and manages a National Appaloosa Show each year, varying the location annually in order to bring it close to its membership all over the country. These National shows draw the finest Appaloosas from all parts of the world to compete with each other in a wide variety of classes. Professional trainers exhibit prize horses for their owners, and while there are no restrictions (other than registration) against entries of animals, it is primarily a "champion of champions" show in which animals which have consistently won in lesser shows compete for top prizes. It is not uncommon to have 75–100 horses entered in a single halter class. Eliminations are held in most performance events because of the large number of entries. Needless to say, a ribbon of any denomination from a National show is very highly prized and hard-earned. It is the goal of nearly everyone who owns an Appaloosa to be able to enter his animal (and perhaps win a ribbon?) at a National Appaloosa show.

A World Championship Appaloosa Performance Show is also sponsored by the Appaloosa Horse Club each year, in which the top performance horse and top cutting horse from each region compete for National Appaloosa honors. These, of course, are not open to general exhibitors, but should be of interest to all Appaloosa owners.

Regardless of whether one plans to show his Appaloosa in conformation (halter) classes, performance classes, or games or racing, the general preparations are the same and should begin months ahead of showtime.

One of the first things to do is to write to the various organizations which sponsor shows you plan to enter, and obtain show rules and class specifications from them. It is of little value to train your horse one way, only to find too late it does not conform to the requirements of the class. It is not safe to rely on advice of friends for these rules, even though the friend may have had some show-ring experience. The Appaloosa Horse Club prints an excellent show contest manual which is free upon request and a "must" for anyone who plans to show an Appaloosa horse. Most states have horse organizations which represent all breeds, and some of these publish rule books for various horse show events. Such rule books are generally basically concerned with a point system in which horses which win the most points in shows during a year are awarded trophies. However, the rule books do contain good information and rules for classes, which are particularly important if the horsemen plans to enter any of these shows. The American Horse Shows Association prints an annual rule book which is available to its members only, and by which all major shows are run and judged. Every professional or serious showman should join this organization and be familiar with its rules if much attention is going to be given to the larger and more professional shows. While it does contain an Appaloosa section, it is nevertheless not absolutely necessary for the person who plans only to show in local and regional breed and open shows. Premium books, listing classes, entry fees and class specifications, must be requested from each individual show prior to the entering of the horse, so that specific information on rules, judging, times, etc. for that particular show are learned.

An Appaloosa demonstrates the highly skilled techniques of a good cutting horse.

Preparation of the horse involves a lot of work some months in advance of the show season. The diet of the horse is very important to his condition and general appearance, and his feedings should be regular and well-balanced. If internal parasites are suspected, they should be identified through an examination by a veterinarian, and dealt with immediately. A rough, dull coat and general unthrifty (thin, listless and pot-bellied) condition may indicate the presence of these worms, and until they are eliminated, the horse will fail to achieve proper show condition.

A daily workout with the curry-comb and brush is extremely important to bring out the natural oils in the animal's coat, and to keep dust and grit from collecting on his skin, mane and tail. There are various sophisticated grooming tools on the market today such as a horse vacuum cleaner, massagers, special soaps and oils; but nothing can really take the place of a conscientious horseman armed with a good currycomb, brush and finishing rag.

Exercise is of vital importance to a horse's physical and mental health. A lot of animals that are shown often during the season are kept in pastures rather than stabled in a barn. Some horsemen combine the two; they let the horse run out in the field during the daytime, and bring him into a warm, clean stall for the night. This is perhaps the ideal situation, although it does present the possibility of him picking up a scratch, cut, lump or something while he's running out. However, the benefits he derives from being allowed this freedom to run outside would seem to overcome any slight danger that might be involved, especially if his owner is careful about sturdy fences and the removal of anything that might present a problem.

If a pasture or field is out of the question, then some other form of exercise *must* be substituted daily. If he is broke to ride, a daily workout under saddle is vitally necessary to his good health and—if he's to be shown as a performance horse—to his training. Lacking both pasture and work under saddle, a longe line can be used to provide the exercise he needs. Muscle development and tone, and good circulation are very necessary in a good show horse, and regular exercise is the main method of achieving them.

His feet should also be cared for regularly, and by a qualified farrier or horseshoer. Many a crooked-legged horse got that way because of improper trimming and shoeing. Do not allow the horse to be without a trimming much over six weeks, whether he is shod or not. You will want his feet tended just prior to showtime, and because good farriers are usually booked far in advance, be sure you make an appointment well ahead of time. Try to have the work done about a week before he is shown, so he won't be foot-sore in the ring due to a recent trimming. If his feet tend to be dry or the hooves start to show signs of cracking, check his diet, and use daily applications of a good hoof preparation to keep them moist and lubricated. Remember that the hoof of a horse must "breathe," and must not be covered with any coating (such as varnish or shellac) that will prevent it from getting moisture. Keep a hoof pick handy and use it during the horse's daily grooming to remove any pebbles or other foreign material that may have been picked up. It is very difficult to restore poorly-cared-for feet to good condition, and whether he is to be shown or just ridden for pleasure, the horse must have good, sound feet or he has little value.

Be careful that your horse's pasture and stable are kept free from wire, nails, and objects which can cut or injure him. Aside from the obvious fact that these might seriously hurt the animal, it is also important to keep a show horse from having any blemishes such as wire cuts or scratches. Although blemishes are not supposed to count against him, they adversely affect his appearance, which is one of the points that he is being judged on. Be sure that the stall doesn't have protuberances that the horse can knock against, causing him to possibly injure a shoulder or leg. If he is pastured with other horses, try to make sure these are not known to be kickers or biters.

Most judges feel that a horse which is brought into a show ring should be in show condition. Many horse-owners have been disappointed and have finished out of the ribbons just because they didn't prepare and fit their animals properly. You might own the best Appaloosa in the show, but if he's thin or wormy, gimpy from a recent injury, shows lack of attention in brushing and currying, or his feet are long and cracked, no judge will tie him. Remember, if you're going to bring the horse up from the pasture just a day or two before the show, give him a few swipes with a brush before hauling him to the show, and expect to compete with show horses that have had daily attention and care, then you'd better be prepared to stand at the end of the line, in the space reserved for entries that make the winners possible.

You wouldn't expect a fashion model to appear with her hair uncombed, her slip showing, fingernails cracked and dirty, and her clothes wrinkled and spotted; and yet there's always one horse at every show that's brought into the ring in a similarly unkempt condition. A horse represents a substantial investment in time and money. The expense of entry fees, stall fees, and transporting him to the show itself represents a fair sum. Surely he must also be worth the relatively small amount of additional effort to groom and care for him properly.

There's some difference of opinion regarding whether or not a horse should be washed frequently. Too much washing too often dries out the skin and coat and removes the natural oils that give him that polished look. However, if he's just been brought up from the pasture and he's caked with mud and dirt, there's no question but that he needs washing. Keep the weather in mind and be sure there's a warm, sunny day on which to do the job, so he can finish drying in the sun after you've toweled him down and not be in danger of catching a cold.

In washing, pay attention to his head, mane, tail, legs and feet as well as his body; and clean out the nostrils and ears, too. Make sure all the soap is rinsed off well before he is allowed to dry. If you can wash him a day or two prior to showtime and manage to keep him fairly clean in the meantime, it is best to do so. This gives his natural coat oils time to restore themselves, particularly if he is brushed well and often after his bath. There is also the advantage of not having to risk a cold in transporting him to the show grounds. A damp cloth or sponge can easily remove any manure spots or other dirt picked up before he's taken in the ring, and there's just one less worry and job to do at the show.

A few fortunate people own a vacuum cleaner that is especially designed to clean all the loose dirt and grime from a horse's coat and mane, and which eliminates having to wash him most of the time. These machines are very handy but a little expensive, and the same results can be obtained with some elbow grease, a couple of brushes and a curry comb.

Before his after-bath brushing, take a safety razor and, stroking *with* the hair, remove all the bot fly nits that might be nesting on the horse's legs, chest and shoulders. Then use a pair of shears (preferably electric) *against* the hair to trim the long hair on his pasterns, fetlocks and cannons. You can smooth out any "butches" by running the shears along the same area again, only moving with the hair this time. Don't be afraid of taking off too much; you want the horse to be clean-legged and smooth. A shaggy appearance will count heavily against him.

If you keep the mane roached (or hogged), trim it now, running the shears down from the head to the withers. Be sure to trim the hair out of his ears. He may object to the sound of an electric shear near his head and ears, and you may have to resort to scissors or a pair of hand shears. A small animal clipper has a much quieter motor, and if one is available to you, it does a good job and most horses will not object to its noise.

A thin or sparse tail is a true Appaloosa characteristic and most Appaloosa owners prefer their horse with a thinned out, shortened tail. A person who fancies Tennessee Walking Horses or Palominos with their long, flowing tails and manes has a difficult

Show horses must present a clean-legged appearance, and a pair of electric clippers makes the job easier for this young Appaloosa owner.

It's a long reach to roach, but this young lady is determined that her Appaloosa gelding will be well fitted for his next show.

time understanding this preference for what they would consider a disfigurement. Nonetheless, when the Appaloosa doesn't have a tail which is thin or short enough for his owner, nature is given a helping hand.

One common method used to thin out an Appaloosa's tail is to draw a pocket knife firmly down the tail while it is held taut by its tip. Another is to grab two or three strands of the longest hairs at one time and, giving a strong, hard jerk, pull the strands out of the tail. The horse doesn't generally seem to mind having this done, and it's surprising how fast even a fairly heavy tail can be thinned by this method. Be sure to start with the longest hairs first, shaping as you go. A pair of gloves is a necessity for this job, for without them, one's hands will become quite sore before the job is finished.

(It might serve some purpose to mention a word of caution here concerning working around and handling horses. The most gentle horse in the world, when startled or frightened, loses every-

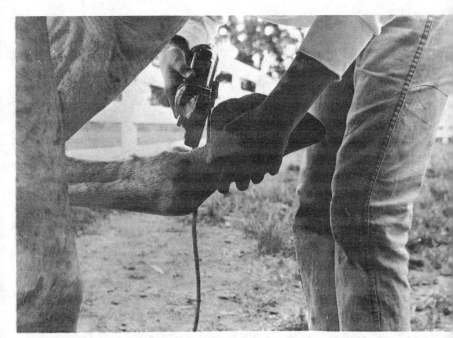

Clipping off the long hairs from the legs and feet of a show horse helps to prepare him properly for the arena.

thing but instinct and the reflex to escape whatever seems to be presenting danger to him. A small dog wriggling under a fence makes a frightening sight to a dozing horse, even though he and the dog are good companions ordinarily. If you are working around the horse when he suddenly becomes alarmed, you may find yourself kicked, stepped on, pawed, or at best, knocked off your feet. You must be especially alert and careful when working in areas such as you would be in thinning his tail, regardless of how familiar you may or may not be with the animal. The mark of an amateur is a complete abandon and foolish confidence when handling horses. Petting strange horses, especially around the head, often results in a bitten hand or shoulder, and it doesn't make his owner very happy, either, since it teaches the horse bad manners. Entering the stall of a strange horse is utter folly, and other forms of lack of common sense only make that person's inexperience more obvious. This is not to say you must fear the horse, but you must never lose a healthy respect for his size and capability to injure, whether intentionally or not. Keep this in mind at all times when handling or riding the animal.)

Once the tail is thinned and shortened to his owner's satisfaction, it should be combed with a mane-and-tail comb until it is free of snarls and knots. The tail of an Appaloosa should fall at or just above his hocks. It should never have a sawed-off look that is obtained when an attempt is made to cut it with scissors. The same holds true for the forelock, which is the strand of hair that hangs over the horse's forehead. In Appaloosas this, as with the mane and tail, is wispy and sparse. If it should need to be thinned or shortened, the same methods used on the tail will work.

An Appaloosa may carry either a natural or a roached mane. If left uncut, it must receive its share of the washing and combing, and care should be taken to keep it free of burrs and snarls. A final brushing with a dandy (fairly coarse) brush, a few strands at a time, will make all the hairs stand out and glisten.

In grooming your horse, always work a small area at a time, first with a rubber curry comb, and then with the stiff dandy brush. Use the curry comb in a circular motion to loosen all dirt and hair, and then brush vigorously *with* the hair. Start at his head, then the shoulders and chest, the back and belly, the rump and hindquarters, and the legs. Clean the brush frequently by

This youngster is getting her Appaloosa gelding ready for a show by removing the long whisker hairs from his muzzle with an electric clipper. The loud noise made by the shears doesn't seem to bother this docile animal.

knocking against the fence or running the curry comb over it to rid it of the loose hair and dirt. After a thorough currying and brushing, take a soft body brush and go over the horse again, starting with the head, over the body and down his legs. As a final touch, a piece of linen cloth rubbed over his coat (with the hair) will give it a lustrous finish that makes all the effort worthwhile.

An Appaloosa owner is rightfully proud of his horse and wants him to present a good appearance always, whether at home or at a show. Because of his color variations, it takes special care and attention to keep him looking clean. Sometimes, on areas that are largely white (such as a blanket, or on stockings), a little blueing put in the water he's rinsed with will make the white sparkle. Take care not to use too much, however, or he'll turn out having a blue blanket instead of white, and this is frowned on.

Brushing or working small amounts of cornstarch into the white areas of his coat will also tend to make the white even brighter, but be sure all the powdery excess is brushed away. A little rubbing on his hooves with very fine emery cloth will give them a clean, fresh appearance, but care must be taken not to rub too much or the natural coating which is necessary to good healthy feet will be removed. Any signs of little yellow bot nits should be immediately removed with a razor, both in the interests of the horse's appearance, and to prevent him from ingesting these worm eggs into his digestive tract.

Daily grooming is more important than just the obvious need to keep the Appaloosa clean. The brisk brushings help keep his circulation stimulated and his muscles in tone. In going over the entire animal every day, you'll be able to watch for any disorder that might begin, such as a cut or sore that needs attention, or the start of thrush or a corn on one of his feet, or perhaps you'll notice a runny stool which would indicate a digestive disturbance. Many of the diseases and injuries that happen to a horse are minor, if they receive immediate care. A horse left without attention for several days might have such a condition worsen until it becomes serious. The companionship between you and your horse deepens, too, when you spend these regular times together, and you'll find that he will enjoy these daily sessions as much as you might look forward to a good massage every day. So grooming becomes just as necessary in a horse that isn't shown as one that is; the main difference is that any lack of care in a non-show horse goes largely unnoticed by everyone but the horse; lack of care in a show horse is glaringly apparent to crowds of people.

If the Appaloosa is to be shown in halter or conformation classes, he must be taught the proper way to act in such a class. Whether he's just a young colt or a mature but uneducated horse, the system for showing is the same and the lessons follow the same pattern. A young colt is easier to teach this to, by simple virtue of his size; he's easier to manhandle. Also, he hasn't had time to learn some wrong habits.

Basically, the horse must be taught to lead from the shoulder on a loose line, to walk out in a straight line, trot out on signal without excitement and in a straight line, and to be "set up"; that is, to stand squarely on all four feet, giving an alert and alive expression. The Appaloosa is never "stretched," as is required when showing an American Saddlebred, for instance. The Appaloosa stands quietly in a natural but squarely solid position. He must be taught to hold this position without shifting, while still keeping the attentive expression as long as possible. In very young colts, this is very difficult, since they have a strong tendency to rear, try to run away, and generally resist all good show ring manners. After they've had a number of lessons, however, they soon settle down and can become ring veterans at a fairly early age.

Once an animal is broken to the halter, he should be taught the proper method of leading, *which is from the shoulder,* not from the end of the lead line. The person leading the horse should be walking at the animal's shoulder so that the man and the horse's chest are parallel. The horse should never fall behind so that the person leading gives the appearance of pulling the horse along. The lead rope should be loose, and any signal to move faster or to stop should be transmitted through the lead line smartly and in a manner which leaves the line loose. The entire appearance should be one of quiet, smooth, effortless action in both horse and handler. This, as with all training, is achieved with hours of patient work and practice spent in the home paddock, but the results can mean the difference between winning and not winning. And an animal so trained is a pleasure to handle and be around, regardless of whether he ever enters a show ring or not.

Begin by taking him in a corral or along a fence. Be sure he gives you his full attention by working in an area where he won't be distracted by other horses, animals or interesting sights. If you find his interest wandering, give a couple of hard yanks on the halter line, and tell him to pay attention to business in a no-nonsense voice. Do not let the lessons become so long that they are tiring or irritating; the younger the horse, the shorter must be the training sessions. Two short lessons of fifteen minutes each, spaced several hours apart, are usually better than one long half-hour or hour session.

Stand the horse so that he is placed between you and the fence. Have a short whip in your left hand, hold the halter rope in your right hand, and stand at his left shoulder with both of you facing forward. Try to urge him to go forward by pushing the lead rope a little to the front. Have this rope grasped fairly short, close to where it snaps onto the halter. The other end should be held in the left hand with the whip, for additional control in case he pulls loose from the right hand. If the horse doesn't respond to the short pulls forward on the halter rope, reach behind you with your left hand and tap him lightly on the rump with the whip. He'll probably run or jump forward, and as he does, move with him. *Do not* let yourself stop the rope or hinder his movement forward, or the object of the lesson is defeated. You must be ready to run forward with him, keeping yourself tight against his shoulder so he doesn't veer from the straight line. The fence will keep him in on one side; you must try to keep him straight on the other. Keep moving with him on a *slack* line until he quiets down. Then stop him, and repeat the process. As you reach behind to tap him with the whip, do not turn your head or body, but keep facing forward at all times. You'll soon have him moving briskly along, and you'll be moving with him at the shoulder, not three feet in front of him, tugging away at the halter rope.

When you want him to stop, give him a sharp command to do so, and jerk hard on the lead line, releasing it immediately. Don't ever keep a steady pull. Try to stop yourself, and the horse will usually do the same. If he still wants to move, repeat the command "Whoa," yank hard on the rope, and stand still yourself. Soon, you'll have him stopping quickly whenever you tell him to, and the jerking on the lead line will be required only rarely.

To teach him to trot on a signal—such as a clucking sound or soft noise he'll soon learn to recognize—start a somewhat exaggerated trot of your own as you're walking beside him. If he doesn't get the idea at first, work him along the fence again and tap him a little harder with that whip. Be sure to move with him if he moves out fast. Soon he'll walk right out or trot out on signal without the use of the whip.

It is very important that the horse learn to walk and trot in a straight line. He must not be allowed to veer to one side or the other—and he'll try to do this. Line up with a fence post or some other marker across the paddock, and force the horse to walk and trot directly to and away from this post. No judge likes to have to run all over the arena in order to see the horse's action, and after all, we like to please that judge.

In setting the horse up, try to get his forelegs squarely under him and in a line. A few taps with a whip or with the toe of your boot on his hind feet should enable you to square them up, too. Sometimes it is possible to have the horse step one of his hind feet back to the proper position by gently pushing on his *opposite* front shoulder. In other words, when his right shoulder is nudged, he'll move his left hind foot back. Keep his head up and ears forward by holding his attention with the whip or by snapping the brim of your hat, or any other means that will give him an alert expression. Sometimes by moving the whip slowly and gently along the halter lead rope, or by gently tapping his forehead with the point of the whip, you can keep his attention. Whatever method is used, it should be as inconspicuous as possible. The judge and audience are there to see your horse, not to watch you perform a series of acrobatics.

The judge has much to see and remember while he's judging a large class of outstanding Appaloosas. If he happens to glance in your direction while your horse is standing with one leg cocked under him, head dogged down, ears twitching, and a sleepy look to him, your chances for a ribbon might be pretty slim. Your appearance will help, or hinder, your horse, too. Don't be caught hanging on the end of the halter shank, chatting with your neighbor or standing on one leg. You must actively show your horse every minute you're in the arena, even though the judge may be looking at another animal some distance away. You never know when he might glance back up the line, and when he does, be sure your horse and you look your best. In a large class, both you and your horse will get tired, but keep him alive, alert and showing every second until the ribbons are passed around, and you'll have a better chance of standing up there with the top ones.

The usual procedure in a halter class is for each exhibitor to enter the ring singly, not necessarily according to number, and to circle the arena, one horse behind the next along the rail, until the ringmaster (or judge in a small show) signals to line up. With all the horses standing in a line in the center of the ring facing the ringmaster, the judge will generally call each horse out in front, ask the handler to walk him a certain distance away in a straight line, turn him, and trot him back to the judge. In observing the horses moving in this fashion, the judge can determine their trueness of gait and detect any faults such as winging, paddling, skipping, dragging, muscular incoordination, etc. Many faults of a horse which are not discernible while he is standing still become glaring defects when observed as he moves directly away from and toward you. For this reason, it is often hard for the audience to see why a judge put down an apparently good horse, or why he placed another where he did.

While an exhibitor is awaiting his turn, he should keep his horse set up and at show attention. This is no time to pass the time of day with others or to watch the other horses. Keep one eye on the horse to make sure he's doing what he should, and with the other eye watch the judge. When you are asked to move the horse, bring him to the front from the line to stand in front of the judge, where he should be quickly set up again.

The judge's instructions will usually be to walk a short distance, turn, and walk back, and then repeat in a trot. Or sometimes, he will ask that the horse be walked out and trotted back. When the horse reaches the end of the course, his handler should stop him in a full, square stop. Then, pushing his right hand away, he turns the horse's head to the right, walks around the horse—which forces the animal to also turn—and they head back in a straight line to the judge. *Never* turn the horse to the left, thereby pulling him around you. This would lessen the control over the horse and it violates one of the cardinal rules of horse showing: Keep the horse between you and the judge at all times.

The horse should be kept from becoming too excited or lunging ahead, but it is just as bad to let him "dog" or drag on the lead line. He is stopped in front of the judge, and when excused, is walked *behind* the line of other exhibitors into his place where he is set up again until the judge is finished with the rest of the class.

By this time, the judge has a pretty good idea of which ones he intends to place, and he'll put them in the order he wants them, moving them from their positions up and down the line. Sometimes he'll move them around several times until he's satisfied that he has them in the order he feels they should be. The handler shouldn't relax or let his horse relax at any time during this process, for he may lose a position if he is seen at a disadvantage; or he could increase his position if he's shown in such a way that appeals to the judge.

Once the ribbons have been given to the handlers of the winning horses, all the exhibitors take their horses out of the arena. It is considered discourteous to leave before all the ribbons are awarded (unless excused by the ringmaster), even when you're standing in the back line and obviously not going to be a winner. Horses winning the first and second places of each halter class will be called back later for Champion and Reserve Champion judging, so they should be kept ready to enter the arena again when all the halter classes have been judged and the call for the Champions is made.

Preparation for performance and game events must start many months ahead of showtime. Some prefer to have their horses trained and even shown professionally; others choose to do it themselves. There is a great deal of enjoyment that is derived from seeing the results achieved with careful and patient training, and the ribbons eventually won will always have a special significance to an owner-trained horse, especially so if he is also shown by the same owner. If the object is to win the most amount of ribbons in the least possible time, and cost is not very important, the professional trainer-showman can do an excellent job for you. If the object is to have fun, working and learning along with your horse, then nothing can beat home training. The overly serious horse owner loses a great deal of fun and companionship in striving too hard to win. It's a very expensive and cold way to own horses.

All one needs for simple horse training is knowledge of some basic procedures that any good horseman knows or can learn. There are some excellent expert horsemen in this country, some of whom have written outstanding books of instructions on training. Add this information to a patient and conscientious horseman with a place to ride and a good Appaloosa horse, and you have the major ingredients for a successful training program. Of course, there are some basic pieces of equipment needed. A hackamore or training cavesson, longe line, whips (both short and long), a saddle or saddle pad and some form of bridle or bosal are essential. If the horse is to be "gamed," three 50-gallon barrels and six long poles set in standards or heavy bases are needed.

One of the main secrets to successful training is patience; another is perserverance; a third is regularity of lessons. These

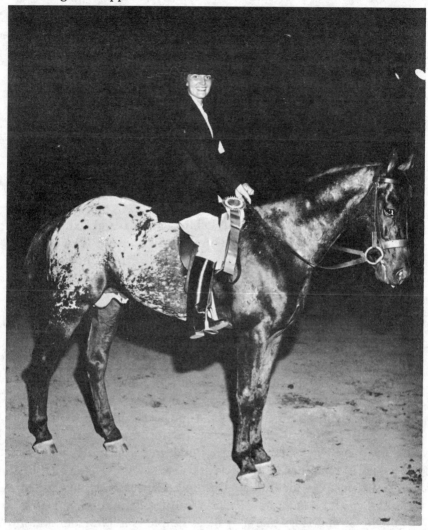

Appaloosa stallion "Shavano" adds an English Pleasure Horse ribbon to his record.

training sessions with your horse should not last too long. For a young foal or colt, 15–30 minutes is maximum. As the horse grows older, he can stand lessons lasting up to an hour a piece. Never work the horse until he grows tired or irritable, and if he is broke to ride, end a lesson as often as possible with a short ride, a quick lope across the field, or some other form of relaxation for you both.

Whenever a horse works until he is hot and lathery, he must be cooled off before he can eat or drink, and before he can be put away in a stall. Anytime he's hot, breathing heavy, and is sweating from a hard ride or a hard lesson in the corral, be sure you walk him around slowly, perhaps with a light horse blanket or sheet loosely draped over him, until his temperature and breathing return to normal. *Never* let him drink a lot of cold water when he is hot, and of course, he must never have a lot of water after eating any grain in any set of conditions. Violations of these rules may well result in serious problems such as founder, colic, and sometimes even the animal's death.

It is very important that the exhibitor thoroughly know and understand the rules and regulations governing the show itself, the exhibitors, and the specific classes in which the horse is entered. He must be familiar not only with what the horse will be expected to do, but also with what equipment both horse and rider will be required to have in the class. Many events are judged to some degree on appointments of both horse and rider, so it is very important that the rider be dressed in the proper fashion, that the equipment be all in order, and that the required procedures for each class be known in advance and understood. In both halter and performance classes, manners of the horse are usually stressed fairly heavily by the judge. He likes to see spirit, but it must be in control and not of the ill-tempered variety. Racing and game events don't require the degree of manners that are necessary in the other types of classes.

Classes such as the Indian Costume Class (sometimes called "Most Colorful Mount and Rider") call for decoration and dress of the horse and rider that may be as simple as a loin cloth and a feather in the horse's forelock, or as elaborate as a fully beaded chief's outfit. These classes are very colorful and pleasing to the audience, and may be presented in one of three ways. These are strictly Appaloosa classes and will never be seen with any other breeds participating in them.

The first type requires that the exhibitors display old or true copies of old, original Indian attire and accessories. This class is judged almost entirely on the authenticity of the costumes of the rider and trappings of the horse. Riders are usually asked to circle the arena at a walk or possibly a jog trot. Since the Appaloosa is rich in history, this class should genuinely depict the part that the American Indian played in this story. The entire effect of both horse and rider is taken into consideration when this event is judged.

The second type of Costume Class was developed because many people felt the time, effort and money necessary to put a good, authentic Indian costume together was often not fully appreciated by the general public. Hence, this second type of class allows colorful Hollywood-type Indian costumes which tend to ward sequins, ostrich feathers and many other non-Indian type of regalia. It makes a brilliant and interesting pageant for the spectators and puts no emphasis on authenticity at all. The riders are generally asked to walk, trot and lope, and are usually judged 50 per cent on performance, 40 per cent on appointments of horse and rider, and 10 per cent on the horse's Appaloosa conformation.

The third type of Costume Class listed as approved by the Appaloosa Horse Club is probably the most appealing to the audience, since it is a warrior class, with action being a main consideration in the judging. Riders enter the arena at a full gallop with each rider trying to make the loudest war whoop. They circle the arena, continuing at a gallop, issuing loud Indian war cries and brandishing tomahawks and coup sticks. This class is judged 80 per cent on action and 20 per cent on the costume and trappings of horse and rider. It takes a good horse and a good rider to stay together in the midst of all this fast action, especially when most participants ride bareback in this class. It's a rare audience that isn't brought to its feet with shouts of encouragement when this exciting event is on the program.

Other examples of events for Appaloosas only are found in the game division. A barrel race, for instance, is called a "Camas Prairie Stump Race"; instead of being run individually against a time clock, two identical courses are set up in the arena, and two horses run simultaneously *against each other*. The winning horses from each heat then compete in the same fashion against each other, until, through elimination, only the winner remains. The excitement generated by this type of competition is guaranteed to turn the most dignified audience into a shouting, stomping,

The Indian Costume Class is one of the most popular events in any horse show. Cal Briley controls his horse with only a leather thong through the animal's mouth. An eagle feather war bonnet, handsome beadwork and authentic reproductions of Indian trappings all contributed to the trophy won.

happy mob. The pole-bending event is run the same way, with two horses at a time on two identical courses. This is called a "Nez Perce Stake Race." In both of these races, the courses are the same as found in conventional races of the same type, but in Appaloosa shows, they are run in elimination as described. This is done to keep the Nez Perce traditions alive and inject some of the breed's historical heritage into today's show ring.

Cleanliness of tack and equipment is as important at a horse show as proper fitting of the horse. To show in a halter class, the halter and lead shank should be clean and, if made of leather, saddle-soaped and buffed. Nothing detracts from a good horse quite so much as an old, dirty rope halter spliced together with pieces of string and held by means of a frayed rope or section of baling twine. These might be all right in the home pasture, but a horse at a horse show deserves better.

Saddle, bridle, saddle blanket, and other assorted tack should receive their share of attention and saddle soap. It is not necessary that new, expensive equipment be required for showing an Appaloosa. In fact, well-cared-for leather that has seen a lot of use develops a lustre that is much more attractive than brand new leather. The key lies in those words "well cared for." No consideration or emphasis is given in judging any of the classes on a fancy outfit inlaid with silver over a good, serviceable one. But everything must be neat and clean and complete in accordance with the class specifications.

Make doubly certain that all the equipment, grooming supplies and miscellaneous items you will need at the show are packed on the truck or trailer before leaving home. The list should include brushes, curry comb, shears, buckets, shampoo or soap and towels (if you plan to wash him on the show grounds), saddle soap and sponges for last-minute cleanups, a length of hose (threaded on one end), and a small first-aid kit with a few of the basic ointments and oils in case minor cuts or injuries occur. A pair of pliers, a hammer, some nails or tacks, safety pins, and screw eyes often come in handy. Of course, don't forget saddles, bridles, halters, lead ropes (bring several), blankets (saddle and body), coiled lariat and chaps (for Trail, Western Pleasure and Stock Horse classes). You will need some clean shirts, pants, hats and whatever else might be required for your classes. Obviously, a small

Chaps, lariat and slicker are required appointments in the Western Pleasure event.

foot locker, metal box or trunk, perhaps from a surplus or second-hand store, is most desirable for serving as a place to keep everything together, and a way in which you can lock your valuables up.

Be sure that every piece of equipment and every item you own is marked or branded so it is easily recognizable as belonging to you. Too often, things are lost at horse shows, and precautionary measures such as a good padlock and well-marked equipment helps keep what is yours yours.

Hay and other feed is usually available at a show, but prices are generally high. Most horsemen prefer to take along a few bales of their own feed and grain from home, not only in the interests of economy, but also because the horse will usually eat better in a strange place when he's given food to which he is accustomed. Although bedding is always provided in the stall when you arrive (or almost always!) fresh bedding must be purchased at the show if needed. If you wish to avoid this additional cost, and have the room to haul it, you can bring your own straw or shavings with you.

A shovel and pitchfork are very handy tools to bring along, as is a long-handled push-type "barn broom." These items are easy to lose to the "borrowers," though, so try to keep them put away out of sight, and be sure they are marked with your identification. Wheelbarrows for removal of manure and soiled bedding are generally available in the show barns for the exhibitors' use.

Some shows provide tackrooms, which are either converted box stalls, or small stall-like rooms specifically designed for that purpose. They are used for the storage of tack and equipment and feed. Some more hardy souls will bring cots and bedrolls and use them for rustic bedrooms during the run of the show. It may not be much on comfort, but it does allow one to be close to the

Exhibitor in a Trail Horse class in an Appaloosa show. She must unlatch the gate, ride through, and refasten the latch, without taking her hand from the gate. A quiet horse is a big help in earning points in this class.

horses in case of trouble, makes feeding and caring for the animals more convenient, and sure beats the price of a good motel!

If there is a shortage of box stalls at the show, as there usually is in all but the very largest places, the use of stalls for storage is discouraged. The number of box stalls available is almost always a great deal less than the number of people who want them. Sometimes show management issues box stalls only to stallion entries; sometimes they issue them on a first-come-first-served basis. In any event, if you prefer or need a box stall for your Appaloosa, an early entry can usually assure you of one.

Water is available on all show grounds, but you may have trouble getting your horse used to the taste of it. Sometimes, by putting a drop or two of wintergreen in his water at home a day or so before the show, you can get him accustomed to this flavor, and use it at the show to disguise any difference in taste.

The premium book for each specific show will furnish many vital bits of information for the exhibitor, from the time he sends in his entries to the time he actually enters the ring. There are as many different kinds of premium books (sometimes called specification lists) as there are horse shows, but they all contain basically the same information. They are available free upon request from the show secretary, and will include the proper entry forms for you to complete.

The premium book will spell out the general rules and regulations under which the show will operate. When you sign the entry blank, you are agreeing to these rules and regulations, and you should be thoroughly familiar with them. Each class will be listed by name and by an identifying number. A description of the class, usually brief, is given together with the percentages and methods the judge will use in making his selections. You will find the charges for entries for each class, and a list of the prizes that will be awarded to the winning horses. Stall fees and any other charges will also be stated. The closing date for entries is generally printed on both the entry blanks and in the premium book itself, together with a statement as to whether or not post-entries will be accepted. If they are, there is an additional penalty fee, the specific amount of which will be shown.

Special instructions for any of the classes will be given in the premium book. Sometimes it will merely state "judged under

American Horse Shows Association rules," or "judged under the National Cutting Horse Association rules." In such cases, it is the responsibility of the exhibitor to familiarize himself with the rule book of the specified association.

After deciding which classes you will enter, the next step is to properly fill out the entry blanks. Some shows provide two different kinds of entry blanks, usually on different-colored paper. One of these is marked for use in the halter or conformation classes; the other for entries in performance or game events. Be sure you print the information neatly and legibly, and that the proper class number and section is given for each event. In the larger shows, the registration number of the horse is required, and the names and registration numbers of his sire and dam as well. Your horse's height, weight, date of birth and sex is commonly asked for on

Squaw costumes are not so colorful as the warriors' parade garments and trappings, but usually have eye-catching beadwork.

a show entry blank. Do not use ditto marks when the horse is entered in more than one event. Careful completion of these forms with the proper information will insure the most efficient handling of your entry.

Reservations for stalls are usually made on the entry blank where a space is provided to write in the number of stalls needed, and the type (box or tie). Make sure your arithmetic is right when you add up all the entry fees and stall fees together in the spaces provided for these figures. If you are sending in a post entry, be sure to include the post entry penalty charge, if any. Sign the entry blanks where it is indicated you do so, and don't forget to also print your mailing address in the proper place. If you are a minor-age showman, there may be a signature of your parent or guardian required on a "disclaimer" statement. If so, be sure this is in order before the entry is mailed. Finally, make out a check or money order for the full amount, and mail it with the entry forms to the show secretary. Do this as far in advance of the show as you can, and you'll have less problems. So will the show secretary.

Here is something very important that too many Appaloosa exhibitors forget to do. If you are showing a registered horse, you must bring his registration certificate with you to the show. While some smaller shows do not make this requirement, every Appaloosa show insists that these papers be presented to the show secretary for examination before the horse will be qualified to enter the ring. To forget them may mean that you've made all these preparations for nothing. Make it a set practice to always carry the registration certificates with you every time you haul your horse to a show.

As each entry is received in the show office, the horses are issued numbers which will identify them while they are being exhibited at the show. Cards bearing this number are then issued to the exhibitor when he arrives on the showgrounds. If more than one horse is to be shown, each will be given a separate number. Whenever that horse is being judged in the ring, that number must be worn or exhibited by the handler or rider. The usual method is to pin the number card to the back of the handler's shirt, where it can be easily seen by judge, ringmaster and audience. Remember, however, that the number is assigned to the *horse,* not the handler; and when one person shows more than one horse, the

This Appaloosa keeps right on the calf while his rider uses one hand to throw the loop and the other to dally.

numbers must be changed to correspond to the proper horse. The only exception to this is in equitation classes, where the *rider* is judged, not the horse. In these cases the number is assigned to the rider.

Some shows will issue each exhibitor a badge or pass, to allow him and a limited number of his company to pass in and out of the show gate without being charged. Sometimes these badges or passes extend privileges of free access to the grandstand for viewing parts of the show as a spectator; sometimes not. These exhibitor's passes, together with the entry numbers, are issued at the show office upon your arrival on the show grounds. It is necessary to stop at this office immediately upon arrival, so that the location of your stalls can be given to you, along with the numbers and any other papers that might be necessary.

Some shows require a deposit of $1.00 or $2.00 for each number issued. This amount insures return of most of these number cards, and will be refunded to you when you turn the numbers in at the close of the show. Other shows make no such charge and do not request that the numbers be returned to them.

Once your horse is put safely into his stall and all chores are done, it's a good time to relax, visit with other exhibitors, walk through the stall area to see what your competition looks like, and generally enjoy the comradeship that is always present among horse people. If you've timed your arrival to be well in advance of the start of the show, as you should have, you'll be able to enjoy the fun and recreation of "horse talk" with others who share your interest in Appaloosas.

Give yourself enough time ahead of your class to give that old spotted hide a last-minute going over. Make sure that your own appearance is neat, with clothes clean, hair combed, boots shined and shirttail tucked in. A quiet, considerate manner in the handler usually helps the horse to be well-mannered, too. The professional showman knows how important these little things are in the overall judging picture, and he will always use every angle

Winning Appaloosa and rider in an English Pleasure class.

he can to present his horse more favorably. The amateur can do the same thing, with the same results.

When your class is called, be ready to enter the arena at once. Nothing is so annoying to both judge and audience as an exhibitor who is late in entering his class. Some shows will close the gate after a reasonable length of time, and those exhibitors who appear after that gate is closed are denied entrance into the class. Keep a close check on the time of your class and have your horse, your equipment and yourself in order and ready to enter the ring when the announcer calls the class.

Showing Appaloosas is and should be fun, as long as the competition doesn't become too serious. Professional trainers are in the position of being obligated to win for the owners who pay them to train and show their horses; the amateur happily has no such master unless he allows driving ambition to become one. Once a person feels that he *must* win in order to enjoy showing horses, he may win more ribbons, but he loses much more in friends, enjoyment and companionship of horses. Everyone who shows horses goes into the ring hoping to win something, and this is as it should be. It is only natural to feel a certain disappointment when one doesn't win. This, too, is normal. It is the *degree* to which these emotions are felt that makes the difference.

Remember to always to be a good sport, whether you win or lose. Remember, too, that the judging of any class boils down to just being the opinion of one man. While a horse show judge is a man of knowledge, experience and background in his field, he can still only give one man's opinion, and this can and often does vary from one man to the next. This one factor alone keeps hope alive and people showing horses, for the horse that wins in today's show may not even bring home a ribbon under a different judge. Experience in showing does help, and quite often the same horse and showman that didn't win the first few times out will start to come into the money after they've had some experience together.

It's quite often harder to win gracefully than it is to lose with dignity. The smug braggart is just as obnoxious as the griping excuse-maker. The respected horseman is one who accepts both ribbons and disappointments without complaint and in a pleasant manner.

Consideration for others is always an admirable quality, and is much appreciated by everyone at a horse show. Make certain you have all your tack, supplies, feed, etc. before leaving home; don't be an annoying borrower. Feed and water your horse regularly and properly. Few things will raise the ire of horsemen any quicker than a neglected horse. Be sure you do your chores when they should be done, and you'll be safe. Always make sure your horse is tied securely, or that the stall door is well fastened. Loose horses can cause short tempers and serious damage. Keep your stall and tackroom area clean, swept and free of debris. Quite often, the spectators enjoy walking through the barns to see the animals, and it is the responsibility of all exhibitors to keep the barns free of manure piles in the aisleways and as neat appearing and pleasant as possible at all times. Be sure stall doors are closed, especially the top portions, when not in use. They can cause a nasty crack in the head to someone walking along the aisle.

There is a particularly friendly spirit of help and cooperation

A colorful display of Appaloosa show horses.

found at Appaloosa shows, and the novice soon detects it. Horse showing is fun, but Appaloosa showing is even better. As one gains experience in showing, just as in anything else, the enjoyment increases. A great deal of this enjoyment stems from seeing the other horses and talking to their owners. You'll hear a lot of information passed back and forth; some good, some bad—but all interesting. It's a different world full of spots and spotlights, and it belongs to anyone who owns an Appaloosa.

6
On the Spot

There are three types of judges at any horse show: (1) those who are paid to judge each class and on whose decisions the awards are made; (2) the exhibitors, each of whom is constantly comparing his horse with all the other horses in the class; and (3) the spectators, all of whom like to compare their selections with those of the show judge. When the exhibitors and spectators know something about the rules and reasons that govern the show judge's decisions, it becomes a more interesting horse show for everyone.

An informed exhibitor is a better exhibitor, and suffers no real bitterness when he is aware of his or his horse's faults as the judge saw them. The spectator who more thoroughly understands how a horse is judged and why, and knows the rules the judge uses for each class, becomes a happier spectator.

So, in the interests of better informed and happier judges, exhibitors and spectators, the following rules for judging Appaloosa horses are presented.

General

The general appearance of the Appaloosa horse is one of symmetry and smoothness; the head is straight and lean, and well set on; the forehead is wide; the nostrils and lips show the parti-

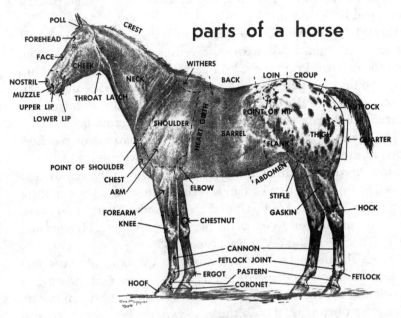

parts of a horse

POLL
FOREHEAD
FACE
CHEEK
NOSTRIL
MUZZLE
UPPER LIP
LOWER LIP
THROAT LATCH
CREST
NECK
WITHERS
BACK
LOIN
CROUP
SHOULDER
HEART GIRTH
BARREL
POINT OF HIP
FLANK
THIGH
BUTTOCK
QUARTER
POINT OF SHOULDER
CHEST
ARM
ELBOW
ABDOMEN
STIFLE
GASKIN
HOCK
FOREARM
KNEE
CHESTNUT
CANNON
FETLOCK JOINT
ERGOT
PASTERN
FETLOCK
HOOF
CORONET

Parts of a horse.

colored skin; the ears are pointed and of medium size; the sclera of the eye is white, giving the eye prominence; the neck shows quality with a clean-cut throat latch and large windpipe; the chest is deep but not excessively wide, and blends into long, well-muscled, sloping shoulders; withers are prominent and well-defined; forearm is well-muscled, long, wide and tapered down to a broad knee; the cannons are short, wide and flat with wide, smooth and strongly supported fetlocks; the pastern is medium, long and sloping; hooves are striped, rounded, deep, open and wide at the heels; the back is short and straight; the loin is short and wide; the underline is long with the flank well let down; hips are smoothly covered, being long, sloping and muscular; thighs are long, muscular and deep, blending into well-rounded quarters; gaskins are long, wide and muscular, extending to clean, clearly-defined wide, straight hocks.

Viewed in front, a perpendicular line from the point of the shoulder should fall upon the center of the knee, cannon, pastern and foot. From the side, a perpendicular line from the center of the elbow joint should fall upon the center of the knee and pastern joints and back of foot.

Viewed from behind, a perpendicular line from the point of the quarter should fall upon the center of the hock, cannon, pastern and foot. From the side, a perpendicular line from the hip joint should fall upon the center of the foot and divide the gaskin in the middle, and a perpendicular line from the point of the quarter should run parallel with the line of the cannon.

The mane of an Appaloosa may be either natural or roached. The tail should be trimmed to fall near or above the hocks.

Most Appaloosas range in weight from 950 to 1175 pounds, and in height from 14.2 to 15.3 hands. Minimum height for a mature Appaloosa (five years old or older) is 14 hands. There is no maximum or minimum weight, or maximum height. Height and weight, however, should be in proportion.

Judges should make their selections on the basis of conformation, performance and specifications for the class. Only when two Appaloosas appear to be equal in type, conformation, substance, quality and manners, should the coat patterns be considered and the award made to the entry which more closely represents the Appaloosa breed with a distinctive, recognizable color pattern.

Any horse shown with artificial coloring will be disqualified and the owner barred from the Appaloosa Horse Club.

No judge shall determine the eligibility for registration of any entry in the ring, and shall refrain at all times from making comments regarding such.

The judge shall award first, second or third place, etc., according to merit. If the judge can find no merit in the individuals in the class, he shall make no award under any circumstances, regardless of whether there are one or more entries in the class or section.

The judge shall disqualify or transfer to the correct section at his discretion any animal not a true representative of the class or section in which the horse is entered. The judge may disqualify any horse that is not properly cleaned and fitted, or any animal that he considers not sufficiently gentle to be shown without danger to the public, show officials and/or exhibitors. Horses so disqualified or transferred are not eligible for any awards in that class or section.

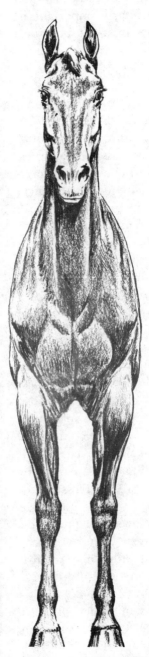 

Horse: front and back view.

The judge is expected to give reasons for his decisions whenever possible and reasonable. This is particularly important in Youth Classes, so that the youthful exhibitors are aided in understanding and learning from his decisions.

Youth Classes

Youth Classes are judged on the *contestant,* not on the horse, and placings in these classes are recommended through the 6th place. Conformation of the horse will not count in any Youth Class. Lack of required appointments in any class will be cause for disqualification, and the judge shall have the authority to require the removal or alteration of any piece of equipment which, in his opinion, would tend to give a horse an unfair advantage. Any inhumane equipment will be scored accordingly.

In all Youth Performance Classes, the judge places the class on the basis of the rider's ability to ride, control and properly exhibit his mount. Any rider not having his mount under sufficient control shall be dismissed from the ring and shall be disqualified from that class. Silver equipment should not count over a good working outfit. A fall from a mount will result in disqualification. No reride will be given to any contestant handicapped by equipment failure. Unsoundness of the horse shall not penalize a rider unless it is sufficiently severe to impair the required performance, in which case the imposition of a penalty is at the judge's discretion. One finger is permitted between the reins when split reins are used. Only leather chin straps at least one-half inch in width are to be used, and unless otherwise stated in specific class conditions, no chain, wire or other metal or rawhide device is permissible in conjunction with or as a part of the leather chin strap.

It is customary that riders of thirteen years of age and under are not required to mount and dismount when showing in equitation classes. Any horse not following the exact pattern required in any class will be disqualified. In case of doubt, a judge may require any contestant to repeat his performance of any or all of the various parts of the required patterns.

In the absence of specific rules, questions of policy shall be governed by the applicable American Horse Shows Association rules.

Working Classes (Adult)

Working or performance classes are judged according to the rules, specifications and percentages described in the premium list. Horses entered in all working events must be serviceably sound and in good condition. Small blemishes due to accidents are not to be counted against the horse.

Ring Steward

A good ring steward makes the work of the judge much easier by relieving him of unnecessary details, but he must not take part or seem to take part in any of the actual judging. When not actively engaged in his official duties, the ring steward shall place himself in such a position so as not to interfere with the judging and the view of the spectators.

The ring steward has charge of the activity in the ring or arena. He should act as mediator between the judge and exhibitors, and all instructions from the judge should be given first to the ring steward, who relays them in turn to the exhibitors. He must be familiar with show and contest procedures and etiquette. The duties of the Ring Steward also include: assembling the class promptly and the elimination of long delays between classes; notification to the judge when all horses are present for each class; keeping the horses moving until the judge is ready for them to be judged; keeping the exhibitors from crowding up in the ring or arena, and endeavoring at all times to keep the possibilities of an accident at a minimum.

The ring steward has the authority to ask an exhibitor to remove his horse for the safety of other horses, exhibitors or spectators. It is important that he be familiar with the procedure of "sifting" when classes are large. After the judge has reached his decisions, and so indicates to the ring steward, the steward shall then record the names or numbers of the winning horses and deliver the results to the announcer. He shall then excuse all other horses from the ring, and the winners will then parade in order as they pick up the awards.

Ribbon Awards

In Appaloosa shows, it is customary to award ribbons to five places in all classes in both the Breeding Animals section (halter classes), and the Working Horses section (performance classes). In Cutting Horse and Calf Roping events, this is usually reduced to four. In the Novelty Racing division (Camas Prairie Stump Race, Rope Race and Nez Perce Stake Race), ribbons are offered to four places, but in the Running Race division (flat or track races), ribbons are awarded to five places.

It is customary to award ribbons to eight places in Stake classes. Equitation or horsemanship classes offer ribbons up to eight places, but more commonly six. Appaloosa Youth Classes offer ribbons to six places.

Ribbon awards may or may not be accompanied by premiums of cash, equipment or trophies. Money awards are never made in equitation or horsemanship classes.

Ribbons will use the following color sequence: 1st Prize, Blue; 2nd Prize, Red; 3rd Prize, Yellow; 4th Prize, White; 5th Prize, Pink; 6th Prize, Green; 7th Prize, Purple; 8th Prize, Brown.

Grand champions receive multicolored rosettes of blue, red, yellow and white. Reserve Champions receive rosettes of red, yellow, white and pink.

The Bye System

Because some of the Appaloosa races and games are run by elimination, the Bye System must be used in order to assure an even number of competitors for each heat. Only when these classes have a total of 4, 8, 16 or 32 entries will the elimination work properly; *in classes with any other number of entries, the Bye System must be used.*

Slips of paper, one for each contestant, are put in a hat. A specific number of these slips will be marked with the word "bye." The number of entries is subtracted from the next highest of the required numbers (4, 8, 16, or 32), and the difference equals the number of "byes" in the hat.

For example, if 5 horses are entered in the race, 5 slips will be put in the hat; 3 of these will be marked as "byes". This is determined by subtracting the number of entries (5) from the next highest of the required numbers (8), to make the difference (3) which equals the number of "byes." In another example, there are 11 entries in the race. Five of the 11 slips in the hat will be marked "bye," because the difference between the number of entries (11) and the next highest required number (16) is five.

Contestants who draw the "bye" slips are automatically listed as winners of their first races; they do not race in the first heat, but receive a "free" win by virtue of drawing the "bye" slip.

The drawing of the "byes" takes place *prior to the first heat only,* but it is absolutely necessary that they be drawn *before* any pair of horses has run. The Bye System is the only method by which eliminations with odd numbers of contestants can be run, and unless it is set up properly before the first runoff, the entire elimination will become hopelessly muddled.

In order to illustrate a typical Appaloosa race in which the Bye System is used, assume that six horses "named" A, B, C, D, E, and F are entered, as shown in the following chart:

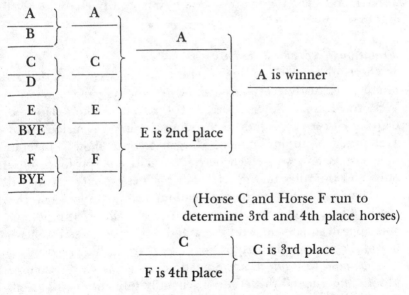

(Horse C and Horse F run to determine 3rd and 4th place horses)

Six slips of paper are put in the hat and two are marked "byes" because the difference between the number of entries (6) and the next highest required number (8) is two. Riders of Horse E and Horse F draw the "bye" slips, and these horses are automatically marked as winners in the first heat; they are advanced to the second section of the chart without being required to race.

Horse A and Horse C each win their respective races in the first heat, and are also transposed to the second section of the chart.

In the second heat, Horse A and Horse E each win their races, and in the third heat, Horse A is the winner and becomes 1st place winner of the event. Horse E is awarded 2nd place. One more runoff takes place between Horse C and Horse F to determine the 3rd and 4th place horses. Horse C wins this heat and becomes 3rd place winner in the event; Horse F is awarded 4th place. Since only four prizes are given, this completes the event.

There are essentially three things to remember: (1) Calculate the difference between the number of entries and the next highest required number (4, 8, 16, or 32) to determine the number of "byes" which will be drawn; (2) draw the "byes" before the first race is run; and, (3) remember to run the losers of the semifinal heat (Horse C and Horse F in the example) to determine third and fourth place horses.

Traditional Appaloosa Events

There are some horse show events in Appaloosa shows that are found in virtually every horse show (excluding game shows). A Western Pleasure, English Pleasure, Trail Horse, Stock Horse or Cutting Horse class is judged the same way in an Appaloosa show as it would be in an Arabian, Morgan or open show. There are some events, however, which are traditionally for Appaloosa horses only, and the rules that govern judging these specific classes will only be found in Appaloosa premium lists or Appaloosa class specifications. These are always very colorful and exciting events, and appeal equally to exhibitors and audience. Descriptions of five of the most popular Appaloosa classes are included here.

Appaloosa Costume Class. Sometimes listed as "Most Colorful Mount and Rider," this event is generally split into two sections, one for men's costumes, and one women's costumes. Horses may be entered in only one of these two sections, and awards are made to the winners of each group. Since the Appaloosa is rich in history, this class is designed to vividly portray some of this history. Horses shall be shown in authentic period trappings and equipment with bridle, hackamore, mouth rope, or other suitable headstall which will enable the rider to have full control of his horse.

Phil Hanson, in an authentic Indian costume, pleases the Judge on the stallion Bear Paw. (Photo by Miehle Studios)

Rider shall be attired in authentic period costumes appropriate to the era in Appaloosa history being depicted. Special emphasis shall be placed on authenticity of trappings and equipment, the attire of the rider, and the markings and colorful qualities of the horse. Prime consideration is given to the overall picture that is presented. While American Indian costumes are the usual, some entries have been made in trappings of the Spanish Conquistadores and war lords of ancient China to portray these portions of the Appaloosa's historical heritage. Horses shall work both ways of the ring as the judge may designate.

Nez Perce Buffalo Hunt. This class is a timed event and is run in a similar fashion to a calf-roping event. Horses are shown under Western frontier or American Indian equipment, and the rider must dress in motif consistent with the horse's equipment.

Steers are used as substitutes for actual buffalo, and 16″ to 20″ circles are painted on each side of the animals, starting from a point just in front of the hipbone and below the backbone toward the rib cage, covering the rumen cavity. The riders will use a "lance," which is furnished by the show management, and is approximately 6 feet long, padded on one end, and soaked in washable paint or whitewash. The object is for the rider to get to the steer and "daub" his lance into one of the circles on the animal's side, if he he were actually spearing the animal. All stock used is numbered and contestants draw for stock. The horse and rider must start behind a barrier which is 10 to 14 feet, and if the horse breaks the barrier there is an automatic 10-second penalty. There is a one-minute time limit on this event, to prevent the needless chasing of the steer. Time starts when the barrier is sprung and

Barrel-racing is a sport that many young Appaloosa owners enjoy.

will stop when the "hunter" raises his lance aloft, thereby signaling that he has marked the animal. If the "hunter" misses the circle and marks outside, he will automatically be disqualified. The rider who properly marks a steer with the lance in the least amount of time, of course, wins the event.

Camas Prairie Stump Race. This race is run in the traditional Nez Perce fashion, with two horses racing at the same time on two opposite three-barrel courses which are triangular in nature. A common finish line is drawn across the center of the arena. The front barrels are placed 30 feet from this starting line, and all barrels must measure 75 feet apart. The back barrel on each course is placed 94 feet from the finish line. A 10-foot by 10-foot starting box may be used, and the judge may start contestants at his discretion any time all contestants are in this starting box, regardless of their readiness.

At the starting signal, both contestants race to the first barrel on their right, race around it to the right, run to the barrel on the left of the starting line, turn around it to the left, race to the back barrel furthermost from the starting line, turn left around this third barrel, and race across the finish line.

Any horse that knocks over a barrel or turns wrong, or any rider who touches a barrel with his hand, shall be eliminated, unless the other rider or horse in the same heat incurs a similar infraction. If both entries knock down a barrel, turn wrong, or touch a barrel with their hands, the heat shall be run again until one horse finishes "clean." If a horse or rider incurs one of these infractions in the final heat and his opponent finishes "clean," the former is declared the second place winner, and the latter is the first place winner of the race. Third and fourth place winners are determined by matching the two losers of the semifinal races. Original positions are determined by drawing lots. If the entries in the class total other than 4, 8, 16 or 32, the Bye system will be used.

Nez Perce Stake Race. This race is also run with two horses at a time, in the fashion originally devised by the Nez Perce Indians. Two identical six-stake courses are set up adjacent to one another, but with a common finishing line. The first stake is placed 20 feet from this line; the other stakes are placed 21 feet apart. A starting box may be used, or the horses may be started

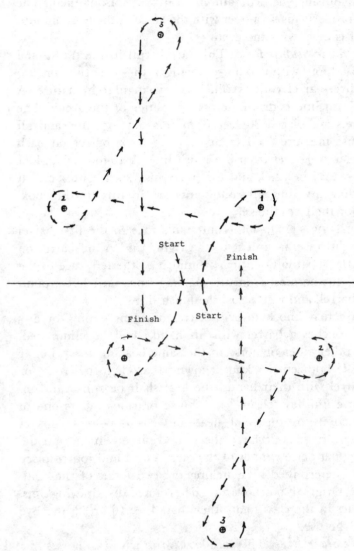

Camas Prairie Stump Race.

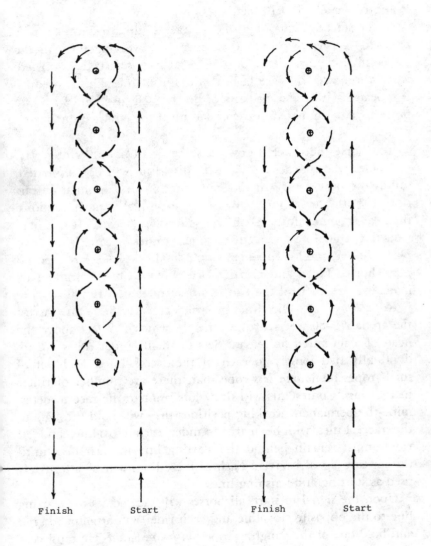

Nez Perce Stake Race.

on a "lap-and-tap" basis, just so long as an equal start is accomplished. Overall height of the poles and their standards or bases is approximately 8 to 10 feet.

At the starting signal, both horses race to the furthermost stake on their respective course, then turn left, weaving through the stakes in both directions, until the furthermost stake is turned, when the horse will race back to the finish line. This procedure is repeated with different pairs of horses each heat, and with one horse being eliminated in each heat, until the elimination is complete.

Any horse that knocks down a stake or turns the wrong way, or a rider who touches a stake with his hand, will be eliminated, unless the other entry in the same heat incurs a similar infraction. If both entries incur any of these disqualifying infractions, the heat is run again until one horse finishes "clean." If this happens in the final heat, the entry which finishes "clean" is the first-place winner, and his opponent in the final heat is declared second place horse. Third and fourth place winners are determined by matching the losers of the two semifinal races in a runoff.

Rope Race. Two wire lines or lariats are stretched *tautly* across the arena, 75–80 feet apart, at a height which is 2 feet above the head of a mounted horseman. Sets of small, 4-foot ropes are individually tied loosely to each of these cross-lines. Each set of small ropes totals one *less* rope than there are number of riders in the class. Contestants will draw lots prior to the race to determine the permanent working positions they will hold throughout the race. Lines will be marked under each cross-line, and all riders must remain behind the starting line in each heat until the starting signal is given. Each of these lines will be alternately used as starting and finishing lines.

Upon the signal to start, all horses will race across the starting line to the opposite cross-line and each rider will attempt to grab and hold one of the dangling ropes *with one hand*. He must continue to hold onto the rope and be mounted on his horse until the judge gives the signal that ends the heat. The rider without a rope is eliminated. One rope is removed at the end of each heat, and the remaining riders repeat the race until the last rider is eliminated. He is declared the second place winner, and the rider holding the last rope is awarded first place. The rider eliminated

The trick in a Rope Race is to hold onto the rope once the rider has it.

in the heat prior to the final race is given third place; the rider eliminated in the heat previous to this shall be declared the fourth place winner.

A fall, or any unnecessary roughness, unsportmanlike conduct, etc. on the part of any contestant may be grounds for disqualification at the discretion of the judges. In the event of a tie between two riders on the same rope, those two will *immediately* run, separate and apart from the balance of other contestants, to determine the winner, who will return to the race with the others. The loser of this runoff is eliminated from the race.

In all Appaloosa races, horses are run with a stock saddle without tapaderos in any humane Western equipment. They must be serviceably sound and in good condition. Riders customarily wear simple Western outfits, such as blue jeans, Western shirt, boots and hat; but both rider and his clothing should be neat and clean. After trying to start any heat for 30 seconds, a judge may disqualify any unmanageable horse; any rider who, in the opinion of the judge, takes undue advantage of other contestants may also be disqualified from the event.

In any elimination event, such as the Stake or Stump races, where there is an extremely large number of entries, eliminations to the eight fastest entries may be made with the use of a stop-watch. The eight finalists will then race horse-against-horse in pairs in the traditional elimination fashion until a winner is declared.

These are but five of the two dozen or more events presented in an Appaloosa horse show. In some, the emphasis is on beauty and pageantry; others stress the training and ability of the horse to perform difficult maneuvers, such as with the Working Hunters or Cutting Horses; in races, it is action, excitement and suspense that provides the appeal. The youthful riders who show their Appaloosas in their own division are always a pleasure to watch and admire.

Because the versatility of the Appaloosa requires a wide variety of classes and events in a show, the exhibitor of an Appaloosa horse finds he must be familiar with all the many rules under which he will be judged, if he wants to show his Appaloosa successfully. Members of the audience as well find the show provides them with considerably more enjoyment when they can follow the procedures and points of judging. It is hoped that the material presented in the foregoing chapter will be a step toward these objectives.

7
Tips On Transportation

If some method of transportation for your Appaloosa can be acquired, it will increase your enjoyment of owning a horse immeasureably. Riding around home—or, if the horse is stabled at a commercial establishment, around their arena—severely limits the fun one can actually have with a horse, if one can just get the horse to where the fun is!

Quite often, saddle clubs or simply groups of good friends like to arrange to take their horses to a nearby covered arena and spend a few hours, riding, practicing and talking. Horse people are a gregarious lot, and they almost always prefer to ride their horses in the company of others. Those who like to show their horses have no choice; they *must* find some way to transport them to and from the show grounds. Trail and general pleasure riding usually means the horse has to be transported to a "jumping off" place before good riding trails can be reached.

The common forms of horse transportation used by individual horse owners are the small truck, large van-type truck, or the trailer. Choice depends on preference, cost and availability. Many horse owners prefer to install stake sides or an enclosed cab-over body on the bed of a small truck in which to haul their horse or horses. A slightly larger and usually more elaborate version of this is a van body rigged inside for hauling horses on a one- or two-ton truck chassis. Either of these are very satisfactory, usually allow sufficient space for feed and equipment as well as the horse (s) , and can be used for changing clothes at shows when the rider needs to quickly switch from an Indian costume into an English pleasure outfit.

Disadvantages of using trucks, large or small, include the loading and unloading problem, the possibility of additional licenses that might be required, and the slower and somewhat less comfortable ride one usually has with a truck. Of these, the loading situation is probably the most serious. Some horse owners teach their horses to jump in and out of the bed of a small truck, but this always invites injury to the horse and is very risky. The large truck will often have some form of loading ramp attached, but because of the extreme height of the bed of the truck off the ground, this ramp is necessarily very steep, and many horses will refuse to walk up such an incline. Either size truck can back into a small bank of approximately the same height as the bed of the truck and use it effectively for loading or unloading; but these banks aren't always put where the horse owners need them.

A loading chute is the answer, and whether it is stationary and must be backed into, or portable and can be pulled right to the back of the truck itself, it is perhaps the safest and most efficient way to put horses on or off any size truck. The loading chute has the same disadvantage as the small bank; it is not always available when needed, especially up on mountain trails and other remote riding areas.

A one- or two-horse trailer is perhaps the best all-around form of horse transportation for the individual horse owner. These come in a wide range of varieties and prices. They may be single axle, tandem axle, single horse, or provide space for several horses (four is usually the maximum). They can be purchased new or used, or can be rented or borrowed. There is a good horse trailer to fit every purse, and it is almost as essential a piece of equipment to the horse owner as a saddle.

A good horse trailer has: (1) a strong, sturdy and workable hitch; (2) a manger; (3) sufficient head room and space in the trailer for the horse to move for balance; (4) a padded tail rope across the inside back of the tailgate; (5) mats or other provision for a non-skid floor and ramp surface; (6) a good lighting system, both inside and outside, that works from the battery of the pulling vehicle; (7) a stout ring to which the horse is securely tied; (8) good, working brakes; (9) walk-through design; and (10) space for storage of small items—perhaps with even a saddle rack included. Some form of padding on the side walls, divider partition, and front of area in which the horse stands is also highly desirable. The trailer should have vents or openings which provide good cross ventilation in hot weather, but openings which put direct drafts on the animal should be avoided. An optional item is a snap-on back curtain that closes off the large opening above the ramp door. Weather conditions and general temperature of the locality are factors in whether this is necessary or not.

The rented trailer will be lacking in many of the items listed, but for very short hauls it serves a useful purpose. The most common trailer is the tandem axle, two-horse job; the price range for a new unit is from $600 to $2,000. Multi-horse vans and more elaborate rigs will run higher, but bargains in used trailers can often be found in the classified section of the local newspaper. Be sure a thorough inspection is made before buying a used rig, however, keeping the foregoing list in mind and checking the undercarriage and flooring carefully.

There are as many ways to load a horse as there are horsemen. Patience is tantamount, since nervousness or impatience on the part of the handler will only add to the time it takes to get a balking horse inside. It cannot be stressed too heavily *that the time to teach your horse to load easily is at home,* well in advance of the time you plan to take him someplace. Almost every horseman, at some time or other, will be faced with the frustrating problem of having to load a horse that just doesn't want to be loaded; regardless of the reasons or circumstances, when this happens, novice and expert alike will look foolish and inept to any onlookers. A horse that refuses to load draws an audience and advice quicker than anything else, just at a time when you'd give anything to be alone with your stubborn friend.

A horseman who allows himself to get into a situation like this very often is just not a good horseman. Training a horse to load properly is just as much a part of the animal's education as halter breaking. With a young colt you're raising yourself, the job is much easier and simpler. An older horse that might have learned some bad trailer manners will take more time and effort. But in any case, a horse should never leave home until he learns how to enter and leave the trailer or truck quietly and without difficulty.

One effective method is to park the trailer in the field or paddock where the horse is pastured, making sure that the tailgate is on solid ground and firmly braced so it cannot move or tilt. Let the horse enter and leave as he chooses for several days. He'll satisfy his curiosity and overcome his fears by this close association with the rig, and if you put his daily ration of feed in the manger of the trailer, the horse will associate the inside with the pleasant occupation of eating, which is some simple but workable horse psychology. This is an excellent method to use with a mare and small colt. It will enable the youngster to become accustomed to a trailer early in life, and he'll rarely object to loading later.

Practice loading and unloading the horse *many* times at home before the day of the actual departure. Put some grain in the manger first, so he'll feel like staying once you get him aboard. Make sure the tailgate is on solid ground so it won't move and frighten him as he starts to walk up. Park the trailer close to a fence on one side, to help discourage him from veering off in that direction. Ask someone to stand near the ramp on the other side for the same reason.

When the horse is brought up to the trailer, it should be done quietly and calmly. If he stops and wants to sniff the ramp or seems to need some reassurance, let him pause while you verbally bolster his confidence and give him a friendly scratch on his withers. Nine times out of ten, if you'll just start to walk up the ramp without showing any apprehension, he'll follow you right on without hesitation. If he does stop, a few gentle tugs on the halter should bring him on, but *do not put a steady pull on the lead rope* or he'll pull against it and rush back out. This excites him, and makes the loading much harder.

If a horse hesitates after walking partway inside the trailer or up the ramp, often a little quiet urging will "talk" him on the rest of the way. A few light taps with a long whip by your assistant outside frequently provides the incentive for the horse to move right in. Be sure the assistant stands a safe distance to one side, however, just in case the horse decides to move rapidly in the opposite direction, or throw a resentful kick.

Once a horse is taught to enter a trailer without fear or resistance, he'll usually do so everytime, unless some unfortunate incident frightens him later. A long, tiring trip without rest stops, a bumpy, jerky ride with sudden stops and starts, or a loss of footing on the ramp or after he's inside, can result in his refusing to enter that trailer the next time you want him to do so. In this event, you must retrain him with time and patience before he is hauled away from home again.

The horse that has become a problem loader may be helped by running a long rope behind the horse's rump, crossing over his back, with both ends passing out through the halter ring in the front. Let the loop hang fairly low so it drops a few inches above his hocks. Pull on the two ends in front, and he'll often come right in. A tail rope is a little more severe and must be used with caution. A small loop is tied in the end of a fairly long rope with a bowline knot. This is slipped over the horse's tail, right up under his croup. The long end is passed along one side of his body and out through the halter ring. A few tugs on this very tender spot, and most horses will resist no longer. Be prepared to jump out of the way, though, just in case he enters the trailer in a rush.

A form of war bridle may also be used to help a balky horse change his mind. It is very severe and a rough handler can inflict a great deal of pain without much effort, so it must never be misused or used harshly. It consists of a simple headstall device that is usually run through the horse's mouth, and which works pressure on the large nerve just behind his ears. There are several variations of war bridles, all of which use the same principle of pressure and all of which are very effective if used with thought and care. Few horses can resist the pressure exerted by these war bridles, and when it is used, even the most stubborn horse will soon be in the trailer.

Most horsemen prefer not to feed or water the horse before starting on the trip. Since a good ration of hay and grain will make the first part of his trip more enjoyable, it's a good plan to feed the horse after you've begun traveling. Have it in the manger before you put the horse aboard, and he'll be more contented on those first miles while he's getting his "sea legs."

Some form of matting on the floor, constructed of a material such as rubber that has some "give" to it, is essential to the safety and well-being of the horse. This mat will act as a shock absorber and helps to keep "stocking" or swelling in his legs to a minimum. Horses that stand for long periods of time in a small stall or in the small space provided in the trailers will often have their legs swell around the fetlock joint in the hind legs, sometimes extending well up to the hock. If allowed to continue without relief, this swelling may cause a great deal of discomfort and might lead to something more serious. Short, periodic stops on a long trip are restful to both horse and driver. If it's possible to unload the horse and water him off the truck or trailer, do so occasionally. Check the tires and trailer hitch at each stop, too, so any trouble that might develop is prevented before it becomes a problem.

If you ever have an opportunity to ride in a moving horse trailer, take it. Once you've experienced the swaying motion, dusty atmosphere and tipsy turns for even a short haul, you'll just naturally show more caution and concern the next time you're driving with a horse in a trailer behind you. There is a minimum amount of space in which a horse can move and maintain his balance in a trailer, and quick starts, sudden stops and fast turns will set him to scrambling to stay on all fours. Nothing panics a horse more quickly than loss of solid footing. If your horse panics in the trailer, you could be involved in a very serious accident. Keep the presence of the horse and trailer uppermost in your mind at all times, and drive with increased consideration and caution.

Always be alert for cars that pull out from side streets and drivers who pass, cut in front and stop suddenly. Trailers of all types are an irritation to many drivers who are in a hurry, and they'll break their necks (and sometimes your's, too) in their efforts to get and keep ahead of your rig. A "panic stop" can send your horse right on his nose and can be the cause of injury and fright, so try to anticipate any such emergency in time to stop more slowly. Much of the annoyance caused by your slower-moving vehicle can be avoided if you will use courtesy and pull over on the shoulder or into the extreme right hand lane until the drivers behind you have passed by safely. Some states have made it a law that you do so, and common courtesy dictates that you will always avoid impeding traffic whenever you can assist the drivers behind to pass.

If part of your trip is to be made at night, be certain all your lights are in good working order, including running lights, brake lights and turn signals. If the horse gets a little jumpy when car lights come up from behind him, turn on the inside light in the trailer while you travel. This helps to dispell some of the frightening shadows that cause the animal to spook, and will keep him a little more relaxed and happy.

When your destination is reached, choose a level, well-lighted (if possible) place to unload. Untie the horse's head *first*, so that he is loose in the trailer before the tailgate is lowered. Some horses get very eager to back out when they hear the tailgate being taken down, and will try to rush out before they should. By untying the horse first, he won't scramble and fight his head in his excitement, and the tail rope will prevent him from backing out before you are ready. It is a much safer procedure, and teaches him quickly to stay put until you want him to back out. If you try to untie a horse that wants to pull back, the commotion caused by his activity could easily result in your finger getting caught in the loop of the rope. This could mean a bad burn or even the loss of the finger. Play it safe and make it a rule to *always untie the head first* when unloading the horse.

The trailer should remain connected to the car or truck until after the horse is completely unloaded and safely put away in his stall. After disconnecting the trailer, the cleanup with shovel and broom should be done immediately, since urine and manure will soon corrode the metal parts and considerably shorten the life of the vehicle. A few minutes spent in some timely housekeeping will provide many more years of use from your trailer.

Although some trailers are equipped with a lock and key for the door, most of them can easily be entered by anyone who cares to climb over the tailgate, so it is not wise to leave saddles, equipment and other expensive items inside when the trailer is unattended. If arrangements have been made for storage of these items (such as in a tackroom at a horse show) it is a good idea to promptly remove everything of value from the trailer and put it all away under lock. If possible, back the trailer into a fence or wall or bank to discourage anyone from entering easily.

Trailers can be found with many attractive designs and options. Some come with dressing rooms, for instance; others with unique storage facilities. But the major consideration should always be sturdy construction and features that will insure the safety of the horse inside. Once you have a good trailer at your disposal, you'll find a large world of pleasure open to you in riding the trails, going to shows and just visiting other horse friends away from the home barn.

8

Versatility: Keynote to the Appaloosa's Popularity

Although he is best known as a typical Western horse, the Appaloosa has been successfully used for a wide variety of work and play activities. There are untold numbers of Appaloosas on many of the working ranches in today's West and Southwest, where their endurance and natural ability enables the cowboy to cut cattle, drive a herd, brand a calf, or do any one of the hundreds of daily chores around a ranch. Known for his sure-footedness on steep and irregular ground, the Appaloosa has gained particular respect from those who use him in the mountainous rangelands of the western United States.

One of the newest but fastest-growing uses for Appaloosas is on the nation's racetracks, where they are becoming a favorite at the betting windows as well as with the owners and trainers of running horses. Long the domain of the Thoroughbred and Quarter Horse, the racetrack now has a third strong contender for parimutuel money, and he's moving up fast. Men who were frankly skeptical of the Appaloosa's racing ability just a few short years ago are now turning serious eyes on the times and records being set by Appaloosas across the country.

Viewers at an Ontario, Canada, horse show were entertained during intermission by an Appaloosa trained to buck "on cue."

Anticipating the increase of popularity in Appaloosa racing, the Appaloosa Horse Club created a Racing Committee in December of 1960, headed by a fulltime Racing Secretary. This Committee adopted and printed the official rules and regulations which now govern racing and race meets for Appaloosas, and has been largely instrumental in promotion of Appaloosa racing under parimutuel in a growing number of states and tracks throughout the land.

Racing Appaloosas may be something new to a lot of people at the racetracks, but racing itself isn't new to the Appaloosa. The Nez Perce were extremely fond of racing, and they found that the Appaloosa heart, speed and endurance made him a natural

Only the fleetest and most enduring horses can survive the strenuous conditions of the polo field.

Double Patch.

for such strenuous competition. Races that sometimes extended to *twelve miles in length* were not uncommon, and quickly eliminated the field down to the fastest horses. The Nez Perce liked gambling about equally well, and the combination of the race and the wagers produced the same excitement then as it does at the tracks today. To the Appaloosa, it's the same old game, and he's still going to the front in the same old way. Appaloosa racing enthusiasts feel that, in a few years, track racing will grow to be the major field of endeavor for the Appaloosa horse. Whether they are proven right or wrong will be told in time; but it's not to be denied that the trend is growing at a tremendous rate, as the Appaloosa once again proves his lightning speed to thousands of new fans every year.

Another form of competition in which these colorful horses are showing more strength every year is the hunting and jumping division. In a sport where endurance, intelligence, ability and disposition are of prime importance, the Appaloosa once again shows his mettle. Although a relatively new field for this versatile breed, the Appaloosa is gaining popularity and the admiration of those who show him and those who watch, as more and more hunter and jumper enthusiasts put him successfully to test.

Joan Amick puts her Appaloosa over a 4½-foot jump.

Toby I, well-known Foundation Appaloosa, is shown as a parade horse.

As a parade horse, the Appaloosa knows no equal. He combines the natural beauty of his unusual markings with the man-made gaits and trappings of the parade horse to perfection. The qualities of a quiet disposition and calm attention to the job at hand are Appaloosa traits that are appreciated to their fullest in this capacity. A parade through city streets where noisy crowds and unexpected sights and sounds can set a lesser horse to spooking is a setting in which the Appaloosa shines. And what rider can resist the pride that comes with being mounted on such a horse! The open admiration of the crowd as he passes by, the feeling of confidence of a proud rider on a proud horse, the enjoyment of a good performance—these are the rewards of the owner of an Appaloosa parade horse.

Since one of the primary uses of the Appaloosa by the Indian was in races and games, it is not strange that many Appaloosa owners today find him ideal for barrel racing, pole-bending, scurry events, relay racing, and many of the other novelty games which are played for sport and for show against the time clock. Speed, of course, is essential for an application like this, but equally important are durability and disposition. It is not unusual for an Appaloosa to be used in an exciting racing event, and immediately afterwards to be safely ridden by a child, or to give a calm performance in a Western Pleasure class.

Regardless of the purpose or task the Appaloosa is called upon to do, he gives his entire spirit and ability to performing the job. His quiet, sensible disposition is combined with a keen intelligence that provides his owner with a wide variety of pleasure and use.

Perhaps the largest number of Appaloosa owners use their horses for pleasure riding on the trails, or in the pleasure classes of

Congeniality and pleasure are the keynotes of a trail ride such as this one.

Rough country such as this requires the sure foot and endurance of the Appaloosa.

the show ring. While many of these will put their Appaloosas to multiple use, the horse's main function is to serve as an all-around family pleasure horse. It is in this setting that the versatile Appaloosa truly proves his adaptability to different situations best.

Trail riding is fast becoming a popular recreation among horse owners, since it combines the pleasure of riding with the talk and

Rest stop on an Appaloosa trail ride.

company of others who share a common interest. Those who live in the lesser populated areas, particularly west of the Mississippi, can still saddle up Old Spot and head for the hills without finding too many frustrating obstructions along the way. But with more and more of the nation's population moving to suburban communities all the time, it becomes increasingly difficult for horse owners to participate in a group Sunday ride without running into the problem of finding a trail to ride in a congested housing development. Because of this, many saddle clubs, breed groups, and other horse organizations have begun to sponsor group trail rides. State and National parks and forests provide some of the best terrain for these rides, but with careful planning, they can be organized in almost any suburban or farm community. Should such a ride take its members across privately owned lands, permission must first be obtained from each land owner, and care must be taken that all riders show courtesy and thoughtfulness toward the man and his property, in order to insure a return visit at some future date.

A trail ride can vary from just a group of friends getting together for a few casual hours on horseback, to a well-organized and planned outing that might last all day or even for several days and nights. If the latter is the case, the trail should be well-planned,

A pleasant ride along the shore of Tampa Bay, Florida. (Photo by Wm. Amick)

campsites located and put in order in advance, arrangements made for each evening's chuck wagon to be on the spot, and any transportation of sleeping and cooking gear to be made and on time at a prearranged point. The trail should be scouted and well inspected for fallen trees or washouts a day or two ahead of the ride, and a time schedule of rest stops and overnight camping should be planned ahead. Such things as the availability of water (or lack of it) can often mean the difference between a successful trail ride and an unpleasant fiasco.

The members of the group should be informed before starting that they will need certain necessary pieces of gear and equipment, such as a hoof pick, some simple first-aid articles for both rider and horse, a sweater and slicker for inclement weather conditions, gloves, hat, possibly chaps, a halter, a tie rope, and a lariat. The leader of the ride should be well acquainted with the trail and the conditions of that particular country, and he should assume complete charge with the authority to make sure all members of the party, humans and animals alike, are acting in accord with the pleasure and safety of the group as a whole.

Consideration for the owners of the property through which the group may ride, and for those who may follow after, is a requisite for a successful trail ride. Such things as throwing waste paper along the trail, destruction of plants and trees and failure to police rest and overnight stop areas, are all acts which may result in your being denied future permission to ride across the property. The matter of fire, of course, must always be considered, and those who smoke should be asked to refrain from lighting up except at rest stops, and then only after extreme precautionary measures are observed. In cross-country rides, permission should be requested and granted from farmers before riding through, and all gates must be closed securely after the last rider has passed. Mutilation of fences and gates, and thoughtless riding across plowed fields, are often understandable reasons why many property owners deny horsemen the pleasure of riding across their lands.

At rest stops, the horse should be securely tied, either to a picket line or to a sturdy fence post or tree. Contrary to the popular movie and TV methods, a horse should never be tied by the reins to anything, and the wise rider will always carry a halter and rope for this purpose. A loose horse can turn an enjoyable outing into a most unpleasant episode for everyone, and it can so easily be avoided through applying the wisdom of this rule. Hobbles are often handy to have along, too, if the horse is broken to the use of them.

Care must be taken that the horse is properly fed and watered according to the conditions of the trail and the plans made by the organizing group. At rest stops, the cinch should be loosened to let the horse relax a little, too, but double precautions must be taken to remember to tighten it again before remounting. Some people will throw the near stirrup onto the horn while the cinch is loose, just to remind themselves to tighten it again before swinging up into the saddle.

No one should take part in a long trail ride until both he and his horse have been conditioned for it. It certainly is most unfair to the other members of the party to have a horse or human suddenly come up lame or sick, or just plain too saddle sore, to continue. Short rides with a gradual increase in time and mileage

The Appaloosa cutting horse "Ramrod" at work on his Texas ranch.

This man uses a team of Appaloosas to draw his cutter through a Minnesota winter snow.

should be scheduled weeks or even months ahead of the trail ride, to toughen the muscles and wind of both horse and rider.

Since the Appaloosa readily adapts himself to rough country riding, it is possible to point him almost anywhere and he'll go willingly. Many a skeptic has learned the truth of this broad statement after riding an Appaloosa up apparently impassable brushy hillsides, over logs, rocks and water, through underbrush and closely growing trees, and down steep slopes. Many horses will refuse to go into this kind of country and some are just downright dangerous to ride where the ground is rough and uneven. Trail riding is a lot more fun when it's done on a fairly open trail or over a country road, but when it becomes necessary or desirable to ride into some really rugged territory, the rider on an Appaloosa can pretty well give odds that the sure feet of his horse will get him where he wants to go and back again.

The rider who gets lost on a trail ride is a real nuisance. In his eagerness to see over the next ridge, or in yielding to his yearning to be an explorer of uncharted wilderness, some riders will find themselves alone at a time when they very much prefer to be with others. The simplest answer to this problem is, of course, for everyone to stay with the main party and not make any exploratory side trips off the main trail. Once lost, the rider should stay "put" until someone from the group misses him and backtracks to make a search. Staying in one place allows the lost rider to be found in the least amount of time; and when he is finally located, it's fairly certain that his popularity rating will be something less than zero.

This girl has trained two Appaloosas for her "Roman Riding" act.

Rules of good horsemanship are especially important on the trail where there may be many miles between the rider and the nearest doctor or vet. Checking the horse's feet often for stones or bruises can prevent lameness. Making sure the saddle blanket is always smooth may prevent sores from forming that result from "hot spots" caused by bunched-up blankets. Riding squarely in the saddle, not hunched on one side or the other, keeps a horse from becoming overly tired and allows him to do his job more easily. These are just a few of the things that every thoughtful horseman should observe, particularly when riding on the trails.

The rewards of trail riding are many and hard to describe. The feel of the sun on your back in the daytime; the silvery beauty of a star-specked moonlit night in camp where the sounds and smells of earth and animals combine into one; the fragrance of rich pine or freshly cut grass; the sounds of singing birds; the first sighting of a breathtaking view—when these are experienced in the companion-ship of a good Appaloosa horse, then the world is a very happy place for one peaceful horseman.

9

The Appaloosa Horse Club

In 1937 there were only a few hundred head of domesticated Appaloosa horses in existence. A few hundred more were members of the wild bands of horses that ran and grazed through the Horse Heaven, Palouse, and Wallowa hills of the old Nez Perce country. These wild spotted ones were the descendants from remnants that had escaped extinction at the time of Chief Joseph's surrender. A few ranchers had become familiar with the desirable traits of the breed, and used them extensively in their ranch work.

One of these men was Claude Thompson of Moro, Oregon. He had known and valued Appaloosas on his ranch for many years. Because of his deep appreciation for the breed, he was stimulated to action when he read a magazine article by Francis Haines which described the inevitable end that was facing the fast-disappearing spotted horse. From the few head of good Appaloosa stock on his own ranch, Mr. Thompson began a serious, intensive breeding program that gave foundation to a rebirth for this history-rich horse.

But Thompson knew that more than an increase in population was needed if the breed were to be truly restored and recognized; a system of registration was required to keep record of pedigrees and breeding programs. In December, 1938, after almost two years of preliminary work, Mr. Thompson incorporated the

Claude J. Thompson, Moro, Oregon, founder and Honorary Director of the Appaloosa Horse Club, Inc.

Appaloosa Horse Club. Ably assisted by his two enthusiastic daughters, Faye and Claudine, Thompson served the organization as president for almost ten years, doing the major work of collecting records and historical data relating to the Appaloosa, and filing, recording and issuing Certificates of Registration for animals found to be fit for Foundation Stock.

With the advent of World War II in 1941, Mr. Thompson's work continued at a reduced rate, and it was not until the end of the war when normal travel conditions returned that the organization again began to flourish. In September, 1947, George B. Hatley of Moscow, Idaho, was appointed executive secretary of the Appaloosa Horse Club, and he has served in that capacity continuously until the present time. From the shoebox which contained the total records and files of the Club in 1947, the organization has grown into international proportions with memberships and registrations in almost every country of the world.

The Appaloosa Horse Club is now housed in its own modern building at Moscow, Idaho, where a staff of 25 to 30 men and women carry on the work first began by Claude Thompson in 1937. In 1966 alone, over 90,000 pieces of incoming mail were handled by this office, and of these, almost 13,000 pieces were new applications for registration. The number of registrations grows steadily with each year; early in 1967, the total Certificates of Registration which had been issued on Appaloosa horses was in excess of 75,000.

The first Appaloosa Stud Book was published by the Appaloosa Horse Club in 1947. Succeeding volumes have followed, containing a complete record of names, registration numbers, pedigrees, descriptions and other important data on each registered Appaloosa horse. Volume VII, printed in 1967, covers horses with registration numbers through 59,999 and each succeeding volume issued lists the registration numbers of horses in blocks of 10,000 per book. These books, containing complete registration listings of Foundation, Permanent and Tentative stock, plus miscellaneous information pertinent to the Appaloosa Horse, are available at varying costs, individually or in sets, from the breed registry offices.

As one of its major and most popular services, the Appaloosa Horse Club publishes the monthly magazine, *The Appaloosa*

George B. Hatley, Executive Secretary of the Appaloosa Horse Club, with his famous Appaloosa stallion, Toby II.

News, official breed journal and "voice" for all Appaloosa devotees. From its beginning in 1946 as a single-page, mimeographed newsletter which was issued quarterly, the magazine has grown to a substantial 100-page "slick," containing top-quality articles, pictures and advertising, and with a cover in color. Regular features include listings and pictures of winning horses in Show

Results, original letters and drawings by children in Kid's Korral, an informative Question and Answer column, and news and announcements from the regional clubs. It is available only by subscription and boasted a circulation of over 14,000 in 1966. Rates are: $5.00 per year; $9.50 for 2 years; or $14.00 for 3 years.

As the parent organization to more than 80 affiliated regional Appaloosa Clubs located over the entire nation, the Appaloosa Horse Club provides literature, aid and information to these local groups, and encourages and approves the formation of as many as can be organized. Some areas support an amazing number of these clubs; California alone is represented by 18 regionals; Texas has 9, and Oregon has 4. These groups sponsor regional shows, sales, trail rides and social functions under the permissive and largely unrestrictive guidance of the Appaloosa Horse Club in Moscow, Idaho, and are primarily responsible for the increase of Appaloosa classes in fairs and major livestock expositions around the country.

The Appaloosa Youth Program was established to serve as an encouraging stimulus to young people through the age of seventeen to take active interest in owning and showing Appaloosa horses. This program provides educational aids, training clinics, a set of contest rules, and provisions for specific Youth Program events in horsemanship at approved Appaloosa shows. Emblems and decals are available to the members, and Certificates of Recognition are awarded annually to young horsemen for outstanding accomplishments in the preceding year. Because of its emphasis on horsemanship (Youth Classes are judged on the *riders,* not the horses) the Appaloosa Youth Program will undoubtedly be largely instrumental in shaping better informed and more highly skilled Appaloosa horsemen and women of the future.

A thirty-minute 16 mm. sound color movie, "Appaloosa," was produced by the Appaloosa Horse Club in Hollywood in 1962, and has been successfully shown on many television broadcasting stations, as well as before club audiences and groups. Narrated by Dale Robertson, this movie traces the history of the Appaloosa, showing pictures of ancient art objects with Appaloosa decorations, and scenic views of the Lolo Pass country through which Chief Joseph led his band of Nez Perce on their ill-fated 1800-mile escape attempt. Exciting scenes from halter and performance classes at the National shows, and heartwarming pictures of young spotted colts, all provide a very interesting and enjoyable film. It is available by outright purchase at $125 per print, or on a rental basis to interested clubs and groups for $5.00 per showing, from: Murray-DeAtley Film Productions, 9000 Sunset Blvd., Hollywood, California, 90069.

In addition to the movie, the club also furnishes 20 sets of 48 color slides each, with written commentaries to fit each selection, free on a loan basis to such organizations as service clubs, 4-H Clubs, FFA chapters and riding clubs.

To encourage the use of Appaloosas in open cutting events, the Appaloosa Horse Club established and has underwritten a $5000 Appaloosa Cutting Horse purse which will be claimed by the first Appaloosa to be listed in the National Cutting Horse Association's "Top Ten of the Year." Other purses of $1000 each are offered to the registered Appaloosa horses that carry their riders to the Top Ten lists for R.C.A. Calf Roping, Bulldogging and Barrel Racing, and $500 is offered to the first registered Appaloosa to carry a Team Roper to the Top Ten for the Year in R.C.A. Team Roping.

Recognizing the need for more and better Appaloosa geldings, the Appaloosa Horse Club presents a $300 cutting horse saddle to the Champion Junior Gelding, and a Bear-Step Katouche Challenge Trophy to the Champion Senior Gelding at the National Show each year, in an effort to promote the gelding of better horses.

Each year, a 100-mile portion of the Chief Joseph War Trail is retraced by Appaloosas and their riders in a colorful and well-organized trek through the country in which so much Appaloosa history was made. This annual Chief Joseph Appaloosa Trail Ride is sponsored by the Appaloosa Horse Club and provides a combination of history and scenic beauty with Appaloosa horses in a never-to-be-forgotten trail ride with an historic flavor.

The list of educational and promotional activities undertaken by the Appaloosa Horse Club is almost endless. Some of the others still to be mentioned are: An annual National all-Appaloosa show; a National point system which culminates after each year's show season in a World Championship Performance Show; sponsorship of an Appaloosa Judging School; sponsorship of annual Registered

The coveted Bear Step Katouche, made by Shatka Bear-Step and presented by him to the winners of specific classes at the National Appaloosa Show each year.

Appaloosa Auction Sales; and publication of literally dozens of booklets and pamphlets dealing with every conceivable subject that might pertain to an Appaloosa. There are guides for regional clubs, instructions to horse show managers and announcers, judging cards and lists, horse show organizational charts, rule books for racing and horse sales, contest manuals for shows and Youth Classes, application forms for just about everything from membership in the club to registration of a horse to race and show and sale approvals. There are pedigree blanks, breeding certificates, transfer of ownership forms, application for tattooing forms, stallion report forms, and even attractive decals that come in three types and two sizes. The decals cost money: $2.00 for the 18-inch size, and $.75 for the 4-inch size. But everything else is free upon request, which reflects the friendly spirit of cooperation that predominates in Appaloosa Horse Club activities and projects.

The Board of Directors of the Appaloosa Horse Club, Inc. is composed of fifteen members who are elected from five voting territories. Three directors from each territory serve staggered three-year terms, so that one director is elected from each area each year. Nominations are made by members of the voting territories, but candidates are elected by the entire membership. Claude J. Thompson, original founder of the breed registry, holds a lifetime Honorary Directorship. The Executive Secretary, Youth Program Secretary, Racing Secretary and three Field Representatives are appointed and maintained by the Board of Directors, and work under their guidance.

Membership in the Appaloosa Horse Club, Inc. is open to any person who is an owner of an Appaloosa, or who demonstrates his or her interest in the breed. From an unbelievably modest beginning on Claude Thompson's ranch, this interest has grown into a world-wide association.

Memberships are individual and are not issued jointly or in ranch or business names, nor do membership privileges extend to others in the family. Active members receive benefits of reduced rates on registration fees, are eligible to take part in the election of the Board of Directors, and receive all notices of annual meetings and other functions and announcements. Membership does *not* include a subscription to the *Appaloosa News*, nor does it include membership in any regional affiliate. Membership fees are

$5.00 for each Lifetime Membership, and annual dues are $5.00 for each *calendar* year. An original application must include payment of $10.00 (the one-time membership fee plus annual dues for the current year), and membership status is maintained in an active condition through successive annual payments of the $5.00 dues every January.

Louisiana's Governor Davis (left) and past Appaloosa Horse Club President Howard Poor (right) make a colorful picture with their Appaloosas in front of the State Capitol, Baton Rouge, La.

The address of the Appaloosa Horse Club, Inc. is: Box 403, Moscow, Idaho 83843. Mail marked to the attention of a specific department, such as "Registrations" or "Transfers," will receive more efficient handling. The officials and staff are cooperative, friendly and helpful to the oldtimer and newcomer alike, and their service to the Appaloosa horse is dedicated.

10

The Appaloosa Registration System

There are three ways a horse can be recorded with the Appaloosa Horse Club, Inc.: (1) registration in Foundation, Permanent or Tentative Books with all show privileges; (2) registration in Permanent or Tentative Books as Breeding Stock Only; or (3) recording with the Identification System which is used to identify horses used in or produced by Appaloosa breeding programs but which are not eligible for registration with the Appaloosa Horse Club or any other recognized breed association.

The Breeding Stock provision is used to register horses that have Appaloosa breeding and Appaloosa characteristics (white sclera, striped hooves and parti-colored skin), but lack a typical Appaloosa coat pattern. They may be registered in either the Permanent or the Tentative Books, depending on their eligibility as established by their sire and dam. They have full registration status as a breeding animal, they count towards the production requirement of their sire or dam, *but they are not eligible for showing, racing or exhibition.* They carry the registration number which corresponds to the Book in which they are registered (Permanent or Tentative), but their Registration Certificates are printed in pink ink. Fees and rules pertaining to registration are the same for "Breeding Stock" as for all horses applying for registration, excepting the one that deals with color patterns. Many horses registered under this provision will later develop an easily recognizable Appaloosa color pattern, and when this occurs, the owner may exchange the "pink papers" for a regular Registration Certificate by sending the old certificate, two current pictures of the animal (one of each side) and a $1.00 fee to the Appaloosa Horse Club, Inc.

The Foundation Registry represents the animals that were originally accepted for registration as the foundation stock of the Appaloosa breed, as they met the requirements. When the Tentative Book was established in 1949, only horses with both parents registered in the Foundation Book, or those which met their production requirements and passed inspection, were eligible for Foundation registry. This Book is now closed to any additional registrations. Horses registered in the Foundation Book carry an "F" prefix before their number. There are only 4,932 Foundation numbers issued.

In order for a horse to be *directly* registered in the Permanent Book, both parents must be registered in either the Foundation or the Permanent Book. Geldings and spayed mares are automatically registered as Permanent. A horse registered in the Tentative Book may advance to Permanent registry when: (1) his sire and dam have *both* passed to Permanent, whereupon the owner is automatically notified so that he can return the old Tentative certificate with two current pictures and a $5.00 fee with his request for the transfer; (2) the horse has met his production requirements and passes inspection. When a stallion has sired twelve *registered* foals, or a mare has produced three *registered* foals, he or she is eligible for inspection prior to requesting transfer to the Permanent Book. The owner is automatically notified when his horse has met its production requirements, and he can then submit a completed application for transfer, two current close-up pictures (one of each side of the horse), the old Tentative certificate, and the $12.50 inspection fee. Upon receipt of all of this, an authorized inspector will be sent to inspect the horse within six months' time. If the horse passes inspection, he will be advanced to the Permanent Book and will be issued the proper certificate. Permanent Registration Certificates are printed in blue ink. If the horse does *not* pass inspection, the Tentative certificate will be returned with an explanatory letter. The in-

Certificate of Pedigree.

spection fee will not be refunded. An owner who wishes to pay all the expenses incurred by an inspector, plus the $12.50 fee, may request an immediate inspection. Numbers with *no* prefix indicate registration in the Permanent Book.

The *Tentative Book* is used to register outstanding Appaloosas from a sire or dam which is either: (1) unregistered in any registry,* (2) registered in another recognized breed registry, or (3) registered in the Tentative Book of the Appaloosa Horse Club. Horses so registered remain in the Tentative Book until they either meet their production requirements, or until both their sire and dam are registered in either the Foundation or the Permanent Book. There is no discrimination against Tentatively registered Appaloosas as to showing or racing (unless registered under the Breeding Stock provision), except that the State of

* After 1970, any Appaloosa to be registered will be required to have both sire and dam either registered or identified with the Appaloosa Horse Club, Inc., or registered in an approved breed association.

California requires that any horse over six years of age must be Permanently registered in order to qualify for State Fair premium money. Tentative Registration Certificates are printed in yellow ink, and horses registered in the Tentative Book carry a "T" prefix before their registration numbers. All Appaloosas of unknown pedigree (when neither sire nor dam is registered as an Appaloosa), must be inspected prior to registration, excepting geldings and spayed mares. All necessary inspections will be authorized by the Appaloosa Horse Club, Inc. upon receipt of all registration requirements and payment of the $12.50 inspection fee. The inspector will contact the owner within six months, or the owner can pay the inspector's expenses plus the $12.50 fee and request an immediate inspection.

The Identification System is used to identify and number good quality horses which are used in Appaloosa breeding programs, but which are not Appaloosas themselves. For example, some Appaloosa breeders keep Grade Thoroughbred or Quarter Horse mares to use as brood mares with Appaloosa stallions. Some of these mares have a known pedigree or at least one registered parent, but do not meet the requirements for registration in their respective registries. It is advantageous to the Appaloosa breeder to have these animals recorded and identified with a number and certificate, so that when these mares are bred to registered Appaloosa stallions, their pedigrees will be recorded for the benefit of the resulting foals. This system also serves to record the pedigrees of foals which are the result of Appaloosa breeding, but which are born without any Appaloosa characteristics showing. (This is not to be confused with the Breeding Stock provision for foals born with *all* Appaloosa characteristics except the coat pattern.) The Identification System also satisfies State Racing Commissions who desire that horses being raced under parimutuel have registered or identified sire and dam. Applications for horses to be recorded in this Identification System are made on the green forms provided by the Appaloosa Horse Club, and must be accompanied by two current pictures (one of each side, full view), and a complete drawing of all face and leg markings. No pedigree can be included on the Certificate unless a breeder's certificate or affidavit by the breeder also accompanies the application. Certificates will be issued, printed on white paper, and using a separate numbering system from the one used for registration. These numbers will

APPALOOSA HORSE CLUB, Inc., MOSCOW, IDAHO

APPLICATION FOR REGISTRATION

(This application becomes part of the permanent records, please type or print)

I hereby make application for the Appaloosa _____ to the Appaloosa Horse Club, Inc., for recordation in its Stud Book and Registry.

(Stallion)   (Mare)   (Gelding)

_____ for registry in the Appaloosa Stud Book No. _____

Please limit name to 16 letters   Print Name Here   Second Choice   Do Not Write Here
and/or spaces

Color and description _____

List Brands: _____

Does this animal have glass eyes?_____ Foaled _____ Foaled at _____

Day   Month   Year   City   State

Sire _____

Name   Number   Color

If sire is registered and not owned by the applicant, a breeders certificate signed by the stallion owner must accompany the application.

Dam _____

Name   Number   Color

Bred by _____ P. O. _____ State _____

Name of the Owner of the dam at time she was bred to produce this foal

Print name of owner _____

This is the name that will appear on certificate

Print address of owner _____

Street or RFD No.   City   State   Zip Code   Telephone

Signed this _____ day of _____ 196___

Cryptorchids or Monorchids are ineligible to register as stallions. They may be gelded and registered as geldings. Appaloosas foaled after January 1, 1967 that are sired by a cryptorchid or monochid are ineligible to register unless gelded or spayed.

Two recent close up 3½x3½ in. pictures, one of each side of the animal must be enclosed with the application. Pictures become the property of the Appaloosa Horse Club, Inc. and cannot be returned. The right side picture must show the face and all four legs. The left side picture must also show all four legs. Please print your name and the name of the horse on the reverse side of the pictures. The pictures are reproduced on back of certificate. It is to your advantage to submit good ones. (See other side for guide).

Membership and the right to register horses will be suspended on any applicant who falsifies pedigree or commits wilful infraction of the rules.

Since January 1, 1962, all Appaloosas of unknown pedigree are inspected prior to registration. Inspection fee is $12.50, payable to the Appaloosa Horse Club, Inc., Moscow, Idaho. All necessary inspections will be authorized by this office upon receipt of all registration requirements. Inspections will be made within a maximum of six months. If the applicant wishes to have his horse inspected immediately he must pay all expenses. The inspector will contact the owner.

To the best of my knowledge this horse has no pony, draft, pinto or albino breeding and is of the approved Appaloosa type and conformation. If over 5 years of age, this horse stands 14 hands or over. This horse shows Appaloosa coat markings, parti-colored skin and white sclera encircling the eyes. The horse is easily recognizable as an Appaloosa. Any horse photographed with artificial coloring will be rejected and the owner barred from the Appaloosa Horse Club.

Signed _____

(*Written* Signature)   Name of owner and applicant

BREEDING STOCK ONLY—If this application is for an Appaloosa to be registered as Breeding stock only. sign below.

To the best of my knowledge this horse has no pony, draft, pinto or albino breeding and is of approved Appaloosa type and conformation. If over 5 years of age, this horse stands 14 hands or over. This horse shows parti-colored skin and white sclera encircling the eyes. This horse is an Appaloosa, but is not recognizable as such.

Signed _____

(*Written* Signature)   Name of owner and applicant

Registration may be cancelled for any infraction of registration rules.

SEE: REGISTRY HANDBOOK   *FEE MUST ACCOMPANY APPLICATION*

See Reverse Side ⟩⟩→

(over)

Application for Registration (front).

use "ID" as a prefix before the number itself. Starting with Appaloosas foaled in 1967 or later, all horses which race or intend to race in Appaloosa Horse Club approved or parimutuel races will be *required* to have both parents either registered or identified with the Appaloosa Horse Club, or have one registered Appaloosa parent and the other parent registered with a recognized breed association.

In order to be eligible for registration in either the Permanent or Tentative Book, the horse must have Appaloosa breeding and show Appaloosa coat markings and have characteristics such as the white sclera encircling the eye and parti-colored skin. Except under the Breeding Stock provision, the horse must be easily recognizable as an Appaloosa. The horse must be of riding horse breeding showing the desirable type and conformation required in a light horse, and except under the Breeding Stock provision, the horse must be easily recognizable as an Appaloosa.

A mature Appaloosa (five years old or older) must stand a mini-

THIS PEDIGREE TO BE FILLED IN BY APPLICANT

Name of Sire   Color

Name of Dam   Color

DESCRIPTION GUIDE

Right Side Photo

Left Side Photo

...ead, showing the white sclera
...e eye and parti-colored skin.

Leg Markings

STAR
AND
SNIP   STRIPE   BLAZE

BALD   RACE   SPOT

Face Markings

SCHEDULE OF FEES		
Membership		$10.00
(Includes dues for current year)		
Annual Dues for Active Membership		5.00

	Fee to Active Members	Fee to Non-Members or Non-active Members
Fillies before 9/30 year foaled	$10.00	$15.00
Fillies before 12/31 year foaled	12.50	17.50
Fillies before 7/31 yearling year	15.00	20.00
Fillies after 7/31 yearling year	20.00	25.00
Stud Colts before 9/30 year foaled	15.00	20.00
Stud Colts before 12/31 year foaled	17.50	22.50
Stud Colts before 7/31 yearling year	20.00	25.00
Stud Colts after 7/31 yearling year	25.00	30.00
Geldings any age	10.00	15.00

The following fees are the same for active members and non-members:

Change from Breeding Stock Only to regular registry	$1.00
Transfer (within 30 days of date of sale)	5.00
After 30 days	7.50
Appaloosa News (12 issues per year)	5.00

Application for Registration (rear).

...num of 14 hands high. Horses carrying Draft, Pony, Albino,
...'into or Paint blood are *not* acceptable for registration in the
...Appaloosa Horse Club, Inc. The result of crosses to certain types
...f roans which have white markings coming up from the belly and
...ear legs, around their jowls, and carry wide blazes, are also in-
ligible for registration.

Cryptorchids and monorchids are ineligible for registration as
...tallions; they may be gelded and registered as geldings. Appa-
...oosas foaled after January 1, 1967, that are sired by a cryptorchid
...r monorchid are ineligible for registration unless gelded or
...payed.

When artificial insemination is used, it must be accompanied
...luring the same heat period by natural insemination in order for
...he resulting foal to be eligible for registration. Artificial insem-
...nation may be used *only* on the stud farm where the stallion is
...tanding.

If the sire of the horse for which registration application is being made is registered with any recognizable breed association (including registered Appaloosa stallions as well as other breeds) and this sire is not owned by the applicant, a breeder's certificate signed by the stallion owner at the time of service *must* accompany the application. Space is provided in the application blank for breeding and color description of both sire and dam of the

The late Calvin W. Briley of Medford, Oregon on top his stallion High Eagle. Briley made his costume himself, and enjoyed showing. A former jockey, Briley often raced Appaloosas.

horse. If the sire and/or dam is unknown, it should be so indicated in this space.

Application for registration must be made on an official application form (white), which is available from the Appaloosa Horse Club, Inc. It must be completed in full and properly signed. Accompanying this application must be two recent pictures taken close-up, one of each side of the animal, showing the face and feet markings as well as the body and coat markings of the horse. These pictures should be about 3½″ x 3½″ in size; they become the property of the Appaloosa Horse Club and cannot be returned. These pictures will be reproduced on the back of the registration certificate of the horse, so only good, clear prints can be used. Slides cannot be accepted, and pictures must not be pasted to a cardboard backing or to the application form. It is extremely important that these two pictures show a *FULL* view of the animal from both sides, but be close enough to show all identifying marks including leg, feet and face markings. Care must be taken that foretop does not cover face markings.

Description of the horse is required on the application form, and it *must* follow this method and in this order:

1. Base color (Bay, chestnut, brown, dun, black, white, etc.)
2. Added color (White over hips, white spots over body, etc.)
3. Face markings (Star, stripe, snip, blaze, etc.)
4. Leg markings (Coronet, pastern, stocking, etc.)

The ruling regarding the pictures being reproduced on the back of the Registration Certificates was initiated in 1966. Certificates issued prior to this time without these pictures are valid and will be honored, excepting those for Appaloosa race horses. *All horses racing after July 15, 1966, in parimutuel or Appaloosa Horse Club approved races, will be absolutely required to have these pictures officially imprinted on the back of the horse's Registration Certificate before he will be allowed to enter the race.* Race horses that have been registered prior to the institution of this rule *must* return the Certificate to the Appaloosa Horse Club, Racing Certificate Department, together with the required two full-view pictures, one of each side, a description of the horse as he or she appears at the time this is done, and a processing fee of $5.00. Fifteen days must be allowed for processing, and the Certificates with pictures imprinted on their reverse sides will be mailed back to the owner as quickly as possible.

Should any Appaloosa change his color pattern so radically that it becomes completely different from that originally described on his Registration Certificate, the papers may be returned to the Appaloosa Horse Club with current, full-view pictures and a $5.00 processing fee, and a new Certificate will be issued. Such a situation might easily occur in a horse that carries the greying gene.

All Appaloosa race horses, in addition to being photographed, are also required to be tattooed on the inside of their upper lips with an identifying number (usually the registration number). This is a quick and painless process, and serves as further means of positive identification. The tattoo is administered by an official representative of the Appaloosa Horse Club, who will record it with the breed registry, as well as on the face of the horse's Registration Certificate. Tattooing can be done at the horse's first approved race where a proper representative will be present for this purpose. Other Appaloosa owners who might wish to have their horses so marked for identification may make arrangements to have a representative bring the equipment to his home or farm at the official's convenience. It can also be done at an approved Appaloosa show or other function where breed registry representatives might be in attendance. Fee for tattooing is $5.00 per animal.

Fees for Appaloosa registration are the same, whether application is being made for Permanent or Tentative Book, but vary according to the age of the horse. Fees for horses to be recorded in the Identification System are the same for all ages. Active members in the Appaloosa Horse Club are charged the fees shown in the schedule; *non-members and non-active members must add $5.00 to each fee listed:*

	Registered or Recorded at Any Age	Registered before Sept. 30th of year foaled	Registered before Dec. 31st of year foaled	Registered before July 31st of yearling year	Registered after July 31st of yearling year
(APPALOOSAS)					
Fillies	— — —	$10.00	$12.50	$15.00	$20.00
Stallions	— — —	15.00	17.50	20.00	25.00
Geldings	$10.00	— — —	— — —	— — —	— — —
(OTHER BREEDS— ID SYSTEM)					
Mares	10.00	— — —	— — —	— — —	— — —
Stallions	25.00	— — —	— — —	— — —	— — —

Obviously, the earlier a colt is registered the less expensive the registration fee. Early registration also permits a young foal to have showing privileges, and his registration is recorded against the production requirements (if needed) for his sire and dam.

The numbering system used with Appaloosa registration was changed slightly when Appaloosas began to be raced under pari-mutuel. Prior to that time, the Foundation Book was still open to additional entries; there was no Permanent Book; and the Tentative Book had a separate numbering system from that used in the Foundation registry. Each of these systems started with the number "1" and issued registration numbers in sequence but not together. Tentatively registered horses were given the prefix "T" before their numbers; Foundation horses had no prefix. A horse that gained advancement from Tentative to Foundation under the old system was issued an entirely different number in the Foundation Book, and his "T" number was cancelled.

A parade of Appaloosas through the streets of Redmond, Oregon.

Chief Good Eagle, with Little Deer up, showing Bear Step Katouche just won at a National show.

Today, the numbering system in use is much simpler and more workable. The Foundation Book is closed. The Permanent and Tentative registrations are issued together, in the same sequence, but *without a prefix for a Permanent registration* and *with a prefix of "T" for a Tentative registration*. Under this system, when a horse is eligible to advance from Tentative to Permanent, the number itself doesn't change; the "T" prefix is merely removed. In the Stud Book, both Permanent and Tentatively registered horses are listed consecutively, instead of in different sections as they were under the old system. This change became effective with the issuance of the registration number 22,000 and all Appaloosas that carry registration numbers higher than this have been registered under the new system.

When an animal is gelded or spayed, the Certificate of Registraion should be sent to the Appaloosa Horse Club with a letter, giving the date the horse was altered and accompanied by two current pictures such as are now required for all registrations. The records will be changed accordingly, a new Registration Certificate will be issued showing the animal to be a gelding or spayed mare, and if the horse was originally registered in the Tentative Book, it will be transferred to the Permanent Book at no charge to the owner.

Upon the death of a registered Appaloosa horse, the owner should mail the animal's Registration Certificate to the breed registry offices with a letter stating the animal is dead and the date of death. His records will be noted accordingly, and the Certificate stamped "Dead" and mailed back to the owner.

A case of spots before the eyes.

The registered name of a registered Appaloosa can be changed if there have been no get or produce registered to that animal. Such a change requires that the Registration Certificate be returned to the Appaloosa Horse Club, with the new name choice and a $25.00 fee. After get or produce have been registered to a stallion or mare, no name change is permissible.

In case a Registration Certificate becomes lost or destroyed, the owner must send a letter to this effect to the Appaloosa Horse Club, together with the required two full-view current pictures of the horse, and a $5.00 fee. Upon receipt of this material, the Appaloosa Horse Club will issue a duplicate Certificate, but this duplicate can only be sent to the *registered owner* as shown in the files of the breed registry. If the horse has changed hands with no official transfer having been filed, the duplicate Certificate cannot be issued to the new owner.

When a registered horse is sold, it is considered to be the responsibility of the seller to effect the transfer. It is very important that all transfers be recorded with the Appaloosa Horse Club. If the horse is a stallion and a transfer is not recorded, no

Here is Appaloosa country with an Appaloosa working horse in the foreground.

breeding certificate or stallion reports will be accepted from the new, but unrecorded, owner. Because of this, owners of mares bred to this stallion would not be allowed to register their foals as being sired by this stallion. Valuable information on pedigrees can be lost in this fashion, and so can the confidence of the owners of mares. In buying a registered horse, the new owner should wisely insist that the seller bring all transfers up to date, or the buyer may easily find himself with a very involved and possibly expensive problem.

If a horse is sold but not completely paid for, and the seller wishes the transfer to be effected but does not want the buyer to have the Certificate of Registration until the total sale price has been paid in full, a request to the Appaloosa Horse Club office to have the papers returned to the seller will accomplish this. If, on the other hand, the seller does *not* wish the transfer to be effected

Ranch Scene in Texas.

These two brightly-colored horses show the combination of color and quality of the Appaloosa breed.

until the entire amount has been paid, but does want to allow the new owner to sign breeder's certificates and stallion reports, a letter authorizing the breed registry to accept the new owner's signature on these documents, together with the name of the horse involved, will permit this. Transfers of ownership are relatively simple matters, but the longer they are delayed, the more complicated they become.

All transfers of ownership should be recorded on an official transfer application form and sent, with the Certificate of Registration and the proper transfer fee, to the Appaloosa Horse Club within 30 days of the date of sale. If this is done within 30 days, the fee is only $5.00; if the transfer is submitted after 30 days of the date of sale, the fee is $7.50. The transfer form should be complete with the horse's name, registration number, sex, date of sale, name and complete address of the new owner, and the signature of the seller the way his name appears on the Registration Certificate. If the horse has been jointly owned, the signatures of both owners must appear on the transfer form.

All owners of registered Appaloosa stallions are required to file

This young colt shows the coveted "handprint" marking on his rear quarter.

a Stallion Report with the Appaloosa Horse Club at the end of each year. This report contains a list and description of all mares which were bred by that stallion the preceding year. A separate report for each stallion is necessary. *Until this Stallion Report has been properly completed, signed and filed, no resulting foals from*

Shatka Bear-Step in costume of a southwestern United States Indian tribe.

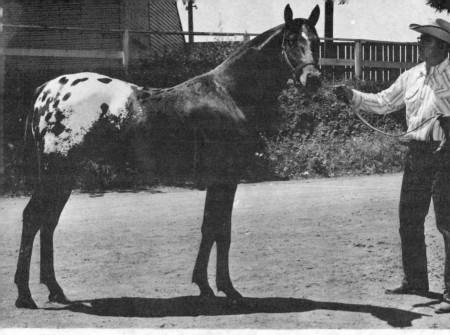

Glenn Moore of Fortuna, California displays his Grand Champion Appaloosa stallion, Ruff Spot's Banner.

Dear John, an Appaloosa gelding owned by Slim Pickens of movie fame, hams it up for the cameraman.

Most Appaloosa shows have a parade as part of their festivities. This one, in Redmond, Oregon, shows an assortment of horses and colorful Indian costumes.

To winter range.

these breedings will be accepted for registration showing this stallion as their sire. All stallion owners should be sure they obtain all necessary and correct information on each mare from her owner at the time of service, so it will be available at the end of the year when the annual report is to be filled out. If a stallion is leased, a copy of the lease agreement must be on file with the Appaloosa Horse Club, and it must specifically state whether or not the lessee is authorized to sign breeding certificates and/or Stallion Reports.

It is customary for the stallion owner to issue a breeding certificate on any mare served by his stallion which is capable of producing a registerable foal. This breeding certificate is completed, signed and delivered to the mare owner *at the time the stud fee is paid in full.* When registration is applied for on the foal which results from this breeding, the signed breeder's certificate *must* accompany the registration application, or the registration will not be accepted. Mare owners should be very insistent that they

Where the Appaloosa disposition really counts.

A good calf-roping horse has to work independently to follow the calf while his rider is busy with throwing the rope.

receive this breeder's certificate at the time they pay the entire stallion and boarding fees, for delay in obtaining it at that time may well mean difficulty later on.

A few of the most commonly asked questions pertaining to Appaloosa registration, with the answers, follow:

Q. Can an Appaloosa be registered if he has "watch" or "glass" eyes?

A. "Watch" or "glass" eyes do occur in Appaloosa horses, although not frequently. They are objectionable, but not a disqualification for registration. Mention of this condition is required on the Application for Registration form.

Q. Can a dead foal be registered and used as one of the quali-

On a cattle ranch, each calf must take his turn at being branded, castrated and vaccinated. The Appaloosa horse does his work well in keeping the rope on the calf taut until the boys finish their job.

Billy Jack Johnson of Waco, Texas, is winner of a new saddle in an Appaloosa Children's Pleasure class. This splendid Appaloosa has a big blanket with a single spot.

The endurance and natural "cow sense" of the Appaloosa mak[e] him an outstanding working ranch horse.

fying get or produce for a stallion's or mare's production requirement?

A. A dead foal cannot be registered and, therefore, could not be used as part of a horse's production requirement.

Q. Why is "parrot mouth"* an undesirable characteristic?

A. Horses with "parrot mouth" have difficulty grazing and masticating food. As a result, they are often "hard keepers." It is difficult to keep such horses in good condition, and they will often require more feed to maintain them than would a horse with a normal mouth. In the show ring, the judge should severely mark against a breeding animal (stallion or mare) that

---

* A "parrot mouth" is one in which the upper jaw extends over the lowe[r] jaw, forcing the upper teeth and lower teeth into a bad mismatch.

Everyone knows Tennessee Ernie Ford, but not everyone knows of his love for Appaloosa horses. (Capitol Records photo)

Branding a calf on the open range in Eastern Oregon.

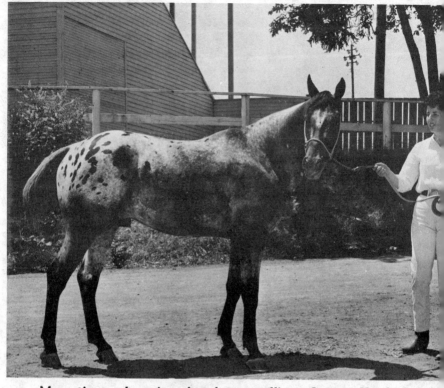

Many-times champion Appaloosa stallion, Copper Head, being shown by his owner, Norma Templeton of Eugene, Oregon.

shows this characteristic; in a gelding or spayed mare, it is not so serious a fault.

Q. Does a brand count against a horse in a show?
A. Branding should no way affect the horse's placing in the show ring. There is nothing in the judging guide which allows a judge to count off for a brand on an Appaloosa.

Q. Is it necessary to have Appaloosas which are registered in Canada reregistered in the United States? Are pictures necessary? Can the papers just be transferred? What are the fees?
A. If a horse is registered in the Appaloosa Horse Club of Canada and is sold to a resident of the United States, the horse must be reregistered in the Appaloosa Horse Club, Inc. of Mos-

A variety of color patterns on three hungry colts.

cow, Idaho. All fees, application forms, requirements, rules and procedures are the same as they would be for any new application, including the two, fullsized pictures showing each side of the horse. The Canadian Registration Certificate may be attached to the application in order to verify pedigree. This will be returned when the U. S. Registration Certificate is mailed.

George Hatley gets acquainted with a cautious young colt on his Idaho ranch.

Q. Does the Appaloosa Horse Club automatically notify owners of colts sired by an Appaloosa stallion when that stallion advances into the Permanent Registry?

A. No. It is the responsibility of the owners of these colts to inquire from the stallion owner or breed registry as to the registration status of the sire of their colts.

The registration of qualified animals is very important—to the horse, to his owner, his future owners, and to the national breed registry where all pedigree records are carefully kept and studied. Better breeding programs with more predictability in colt crops can be the result of an intensive examination of the genetic material available through registration records. Because a permanent

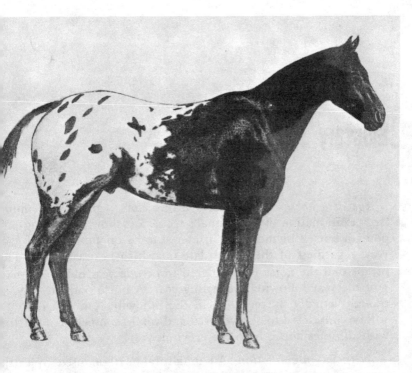

Drawing of a typical blanket-type Appaloosa.

ecord is kept of each horse's name, number, sex, description, color, ate of birth, pedigree, name of breeder, and names and addresses f each owner, both the buyer and seller of this animal are afforded rotection against fraud and misrepresentation. Breed registration emoves an animal from a "grade" level to one of acceptance. 'he owner of a registered horse is allowed pleasures and privileges, ich as participation in certain sporting events for example, that e grade horse owner is not permitted to enjoy. The Registration 'ertificate officially declares the horse's pedigree and quality, and e Appaloosa owner takes pride in owning the horse which carries

Glossary

Age of a horse. The actual age of a horse can be determined from examination of the animal's teeth. For show and racing purposes, a horse's birthday is considered to be on January 1 of each year, regardless of the actual date on which he was foaled. This means that the horse is considered to be one year old on January 1 of the year following his foaling year. A horse born in July, although actually six months' old the following January 1, would still be considered to be a year old and would compete as a yearling with all other horses born the previous year.

Artificial insemination. An unnatural method used by cattlemen, and to a lesser degree by horse breeders, to impregnate the female with semen from a male of outstanding bloodlines for purposes of producing offspring.

Bald face. A white facing marking that covers most of the front of the head of the horse, and often extends into the cheeks on the sides.

Bay. A common, reddish-brown color which ranges from a bright, cherry red through mahogany to a deep, dark shade. Bay colored horses will always have black points. Sometimes the color of light bay and a sorrel are very much alike, but they are easily distinguishable since a bay always has black points and a sorrel's points are the same color as his coat.

Bear Step Katouche. A special award, highly-prized by Appaloosa owners, which is handcrafted from solid silver and turquoise by Shatka Bear-Step and donated by him to the Appaloosa Horse

A brightly marked pair of Appaloosas bearing the leopard type of coat pattern.

Notice the shading or "halo" effect around the spots in this stallion's blanket. This is typical of many Appaloosa markings.

Betty R. Marble
58

Club for presentation to specific class winners at the National Show each year.

Blaze. A broad white face marking.

Blemish. A mark or scar which is not inherited and does not affect the soundness of a horse or his ability to function in any way.

Bolt. To run away. A horse that is bolting will not respond to the bit or legs. The action can be caused by momentary fright, or may be an established vice. In either case, only an experienced horseman should be allowed to ride the horse until the animal has been cured of the habit.

Boot. A white leg marking that extends from the hoof to the lower half of the cannon just above the fetlock joint. Also called a "Half Stocking." When the marking reaches just over the fetlock, it is called an "Ankle."

Bosal. An elliptical noseband made of braided rawhide with a heavy "heel" knot that is carried just under and behind the horse's jaw. When fitted with a headstall and mecate, it is commonly known as a "Spanish hackamore," and is used as a training device as well as a substitute for a bridle and bit. Control by the rider is achieved by causing the noseband to press against the nose of the horse, thereby cutting off his wind. The hind heel knot can be brought up to sharply strike the tender area behind and under the jaw. It comes in various sizes and diameters, and is an effective, yet humane, piece of equipment used for many years by experienced Spanish and Mexican horsemen.

Bot fly. A fly common to horse barns and pastures which lays its tiny yellow eggs on the leg, shoulder, nose and throat hair of horses during the summer months. The horse will ingest these eggs into his digestive tract where they hatch larvae which live and feed from the lining of the stomach. The bot larvae will live for months in the stomach of the horse, causing a great drain on the animal and often resulting in digestive disturbances and colic. The horse quickly becomes poor and unthrifty. The larvae of the bot fly are called "worms" or "bots" by most horsemen, and their removal requires the aid of a veterinarian.

Bowline knot. One of the few knots in which the loop does not get smaller when a pull is applied, making it a very useful knot for anyone to know who works around horses.

Brand. An identifying mark which is imprinted into the hide of an animal by means of a hot iron. Used principally by Western cattlemen and horsemen to mark their stock, a brand may be of

Betty Marble

any design but must be registered and issued to its owner, and must be put only on the area of the animal designated by the registration. Spanish brands were often extremely large and intricate, while those of the western United States are usually made up of a simple combination of letters and/or geometric figures such as squares, triangles and circles. A brand on an Appaloosa is not counted against him in a show.

Brood mare. A mare whose chief function is to produce healthy foals in a horseman's breeding program.

Buck. Action of a horse designed to unseat his rider, which ranges from simple "crow-hopping" to full-fledged "sun-fishing" with the horse's head down between his knees and his heels stretched to the sky. A young horse may indulge in such antics out of spirit, but when a horse engages in these activities often and persistently, an experienced trainer is needed to teach him manners.

Cavesson. A heavy leather noseband strap which is fitted with sturdy metal rings and is attached to a headstall for use by trainers to teach a horse basic maneuvers, manners and reining from the ground.

Chestnut. A very deep, dark reddish sorrel. Sorrel-colored Thoroughbreds are always designated as "chestnut." Points of a chestnut or sorrel-colored horse are the same reddish color as the body hair.

Colic. A digestive disturbance which is symptomatic of some internal trouble, such as indigestion, looped intestine, worms or bad feed. The horse appears sick, bloated, sweating and obviously in great discomfort. He usually bites at his flank, and lies down and gets up a great deal. A vet should be called, and the horse kept on his feet and walking until help arrives.

Collected. A horse which is balanced and has his legs well under him is collected. His head is nearly vertical, not extended outward, and he is ready to move and respond to the rider's directions and signals. The rider collects his horse by using his legs strongly to drive the horse's hindquarters under him, while the rider keeps a light check on the mouth with the reins to stop or check the forward propulsion. A good rider will collect his horse before starting, stopping, or changing gait or movement.

Colt. A young male horse from the time he is weaned until he reaches five years of age. This term is frequently incorrectly used to denote a young horse of either sex, but females of the same age should properly be called "fillies." Prior to weaning, colts and fillies are both known as "foals." After weaning, the male may be named a "weanling colt," a "yearling colt," etc. until he is five years old. For show purposes, however, a horse is considered to be "aged" at four years of age.

Conformation. The body structure or shape (of a horse).

Corn. A bruise which occurs on a horse's foot and which is caused by injury to the sole resulting in inflammation of the horn, and generally found between the bars and the hoof wall. The area will be discolored and is tender, often causing the horse to become lame.

Coupling. The distance between the top of the hip joint and the top of the shoulder joint, or the space between the hindquarters and the frontquarters. Most horsemen prefer that their riding horses be short-coupled, but some breeders desire a little longer coupling in a brood mare to provide more room for an unborn foal.

Coup Stick. To the American Indian, a "coup" (pronounced "coo") was a trophy of scalp or feathers which represented an enemy he had killed with his own hands. A coup stick was a light pole about five or six feet high to which the feathers or scalps were fastened. The more coups on the stick, the greater the warrior. These coup sticks were attached to the lodge pole of the teepee, or carried by the mounted Indian as proof of his bravery in battle. Replicas of the coup sticks are often carried as part of the trappings of an exhibitor in an Appaloosa Indian Costume class in modern horse shows.

Cross-firing. A term used to describe a horse's action when, at a trot or lope, his feet strike each other in the air. This term should *not* be erroneously applied to mean a disunited horse.

Cryptorchid. A male whose testicles have not descended into the scrotum. Sometimes called a "double cryptorchid."

Cutting horse. A well-trained horse used at branding time to separate a cow and her calf. The horse must enter a herd quietly, and after the rider indicates which calf is wanted, the horse works independently to cut the calf away from the herd and keep it from running back until it has been roped or turned into a corral. These horses must have natural ability (horsemen call it "cow sense") and the natural desire to "work" cattle. They are highly prized, both by working stockmen and by showmen who exhibit cutting horses in the show arena.

Dam. Proper term to denote a horse's mother. A colt is said to be *out of* his dam; he is *by* his sire. Good horsemen will always say "out of" when speaking of the dam or mother, and "by" when designating the sire or father, never in reverse.

Disunited. When, in a lope, a horse takes one lead with his front legs, and the opposite lead with his hind legs, he is said to be disunited.

Dun. A shade of yellow mixed with other colors to form variations from pale, creamy gold to a dingy, dirty tan. When the yellow is mixed with white hairs, the dun is cream or gold-colored, such as a criollo or Palomino. These horses always have white points, never black. If the yellow is mixed with red (sorrel), he is called a "claybank" and has red points. If the yellow is mixed with bay, the horse is called a "buckskin." He always has black points and often carries a black line down the center of his back, thus becoming a "lineback buckskin." If the yellow hairs are mixed with brown or black, the horse is a "grulla" (pronounced "grew-ya") and is a blue-grey mouse color.

Equitation. The skill of proper horsemanship in riding. Equitation classes are those in which the ability and performance of the *rider* is judged, rather than the horse.

Exhibitor. The person who shows or exhibits a horse in competition (not necessarily the owner of the horse).

Betty Marble

Farrier. A highly-skilled and trained professional horseshoer.

Filly. Proper term for a young *female* horse from the time she is weaned until she reaches 5 years of age. Prior to weaning, she is called a "foal." After weaning she is called a "weanling filly," a "yearling filly," etc. until she is five years old when she becomes a "mare." For show purposes, however, a female horse is considered "aged" at 4 years, and classes are so designated.

Foal. A term used to designate a young horse of either sex from the time of birth until weaned from the dam.

Founder (Laminitis). A very serious disease which affects the feet of a horse and is commonly caused by improper feeding or over-feeding, especially of grain, or by hard usage on pavement

or cement. The tissues in the feet swell, but being encased by the hard hoof, they cannot expand. This causes extremely painful pressure and heat, and the affected horse will tremble and refuse to walk or move, exhibiting obvious signs of pain when forced to do so. Immediate treatment must be given to prevent permanently deformed feet and lameness. They should be soaked at once in cold water, with ice if possible, and a vet called at once to administer drugs and treatment.

Gelding. A male horse which has been altered (castrated), and which is not capable of siring colts.

Genes. Elements containing inheritable factors—such as color of eyes, height, disposition, etc.—which may be dominant or recessive and which are passed onto the offspring in specific combinations with the genes of the other parent.

Genetics. The biological science that deals with the study of heredity.

Gestation. Term of pregnancy.

Get. Term properly applied to the foals which are sired by a stallion.

Gimpy. Slang expression for a limping or lame horse.

Glass eye. Also called "watch eye." An eye in which there is an absence of pigment in the iris, causing the eye to appear to be blue, rather than the usual brown or hazel. While this condition in no way affects the sight or vision of the horse, glass eyes are considered to be undesirable in most horses including Appaloosas.

Grade horse. A horse which does not carry enough blood or characteristics of any specific breed in sufficient quantities to meet registration requirements. Sometimes applied to a horse with one registered parent and the other of common stock.

Gymkhana. Competitive games played on horseback.

Hackamore. A bridle which does not use a bit or any device that is placed inside the horse's mouth. Control is achieved through pressure on the animal's nose.

Hand. A measurement of a horse's height which is equal to four inches. A horse that stands 15 hands high is 60 inches or 5 feet tall at his withers.

Betty Marble '58

Headstall. That part of a bridle or hackamore which fits over a horse's head for the purpose of holding a bit, bosal or similar device in the horse's mouth or on his nose, and to which the reins are attached. Some headstalls are very light and of simple construction; others may be made of wide straps which are heavily decorated with nickel or silver ornaments.

Heat (in mares). Also known as "season." The period in which a mare will accept a stallion for breeding and in which pregnancy can result. An average mare will "come in heat" every 18–21 days, usually with more regularity during the spring and summer months, and this period will continue for 3–5 days. Once pregnant, most mares will discontinue having "heat" periods until approximately 9 days after the birth of the foal. Exceptions do occur in which mares have regular heat cycles throughout their pregnancies, and because of this, an examination by a veterinarian 45 days or more following service is the only positive method of determining whether or not a mare has conceived to that service.

Heat (in games). A sub-contest in a race. A runoff. Some racing events require that the horses compete several times in elimination rounds or "heats" prior to the final heat in which the winner of the event is determined.

In-breeding. Mating of close relatives, such as father-to-daughter, brother-to-sister, etc. A practice in which there is a high risk of producing offspring with poor dispositions and other faults, in the gamble of perhaps obtaining a foal of outstanding quality. It is seldom used in horse breeding programs.

Line-breeding. Mating of animals which have a common ancestor, several generations removed, such as the mating of a mare to her grandfather or great-grandfather, or a stallion to his aunt, etc. It is practiced for the same reasons as in-breeding is used, in the hope that the resulting foal will show concentration of the best qualities of the bloodline. Unfortunately, in most line-bred foals, it is the poor qualities that become concentrated. Line-breeding presents the same dangers that occur in programs using in-breeding, but slightly less intensified.

Longe line. A rope or piece of webbing, 20–30 feet long, with a sturdy snap fastened in one end. The longe (not "lunge") line is attached to the halter or training cavesson of a horse and is used for training and exercising the animal from the ground.

Mare. A mature female horse.

Mature horse. A horse of any sex which has reached five years of age, at which time his mouth is said to be "made" or "full."

Monorchid. Sometimes called a "single cryptorchid" or "ridgling." A male in which one testicle has dropped into the scrotum, and one is still retained in the abdominal cavity.

Near side. The left side of a horse.

Off side. The right side of a horse.

Open mare. Sometimes called a "yeld" mare. A mare which is not pregnant or carrying a foal.

Out-crossing (or cross-breeding). The mating of two registered purebred horses from two different breeds.

Paddling. A horse that throws his feet in wide, outward arcs when he moves is said to be "paddling." It is common in pigeon-toed horses.

Paddock. A pasture-lot or field adjoining a stable, completely enclosed by good fence (usually wooden) in which horses are kept or exercised. It may be as small as just a few square yards, or as large as several acres.

Palomino. A horse which is registered on the basis of color only. This horse must have a cream- or golden-colored coat, dark skin, and white or silvery points (never black). He may be of any breed or combination of breeds, but the Arabians, Thoroughbreds and American Saddle Horses are most popularly used. The Palomino is often used as a parade horse.

Parasites. The most common external parasites in horses are horse lice and mites. These can both cause intense itching, scaling, loss of hair, and a poor appearance in general. There are several medications and treatments available for their removal. Internal parasites most common to horses are the stomach and intestinal worms known as bots, ascarids, strongyles (or bloodworms) and pinworms. A horse infested with worms has a rough coat, is listless, pot-bellied, and generally unthrifty. Various treatments may be used to rid the horse of the parasites, but it is necessary to repeat the treatment at regular intervals in order to keep the animal fairly free of them. A large infestation may cause intestinal impaction and could result in the eventual death of the horse.

Parimutuel. A system of betting used at racetracks which, in its simplest form, means that all the money from all the bets is pooled. A percentage is taken off by the operators of the system, and the balance is divided up among the people who bet on the winning horses, according to the odds on each. Odds are calculated automatically by machine, and indicate the number of bets that are placed on each horse; the more bets placed, the lower the odds and the less amount of money won if the horse wins; and vice-versa.

Pedigree. An animal's family tree or record of ancestry. The ancestry of the sire (or father) is called the "top line"; that of the dam (or mother) is called the "bottom line." This is because the sire is traditionally written on the top line of a pedigree chart, and the name of the dam is put on the bottom line.

Points. The points of a horse refer to his mane and tail, specifically the color of the mane and tail.

Produce. The offspring from a mare. A foal is the *produce* of a mare, and the *get* of a stallion.

Race. A narrow strip of white marking that runs at an angle across the face of a horse.

Roach. To cut or shear a horse's mane very short, leaving the foretop and a wisp of long hair as a hand-hold at the withers. Originally, the term "roach" meant to cut the mane, but leaving it several inches high. Today, this is called a "pony roach." Most Western horses are roached.

Roan. The color of a horse's coat when white hairs are mixed with the base coat color. A bay mixed with white becomes a red roan; a sorrel mixed with white is a strawberry roan; and a black mixed with white is a blue roan. Some roans are mostly white, and are known as "flea-bitten." All grey horses are technically roans.

Sclera. The white substance in an eye that surrounds the iris. This is a characteristic feature of the human eye, and of the eye of the Appaloosa horse.

Settle. A mare is said to "settle" or "settle to service" when she conceives from a mating.

Sifting. A method used in horse shows with very large classes, where the judge will ask that the class be divided into several groups from which he will make selections. These selections, from the "first sift," the "second sift," etc., are then judged together as a single class, and the balance of the horses are excused from the arena.

Sire. The male parent (or father) of a horse. A colt is said to be *by* his sire, and *out of* his dam, never the other way around.

Slack. Looseness, as in a rope hanging loose.

Snip. A small patch of white on a horse's muzzle that often will extend into the lip.

MARILYN J. KITCH
'58

Sock. A short, white marking on a horse's foot, extending along his pastern to, (but not including) the fetlock joint. Also called a "pastern." When it extends only half-way along the pastern, it is called a "half-pastern"; when it consists of just a narrow band of white along the top of the hoof, it is called a "coronet."

Sorrel. A reddish-colored coat on a horse. A sorrel horse has red points which are the same shade as his coat color. If his points are white or cream-colored, he is called a "Ysabella" or "flaxen sorrel." A sorrel horse never has a black mane or tail.

Sound. A sound horse is free from impairment of wind, legs, eyes, ears, action or any unsoundness. An unsoundness is something that adversely affects the horse's use or function, such as ringbone, thoroughpin, bowed tendon, heaves, spavin, etc., and can be inherited or received from injury.

Spayed mare. A mare which has had her ovaries removed by surgery and is no longer capable of producing a foal.

Stallion. A mature, male horse which is capable of siring foals.

Star. A patch of white on a horse's forehead, roughly the size of a quarter or larger. A smaller similar marking would be called a "spot."

Stock horse. A horse trained to work and herd cattle. Whether on a ranch or in a Stock Horse class in a horse show, he must be able to turn quickly and lightly on his hindquarters, respond well to light reining, be able to change direction quickly, be capable of short bursts of speed and sudden, collected stops, and always be in balance. He is the product of natural ability and many hours of training.

Stocking. A white leg marking that extends from the hoof to above the middle of the cannon bone, or to just below the knee or hock joint. Also called a "full stocking."

Stripe. Long, narrow, white face marking which runs in a fairly straight line from the top of a horse's forehead to or almost to the muzzle.

Striped hoof. An Appaloosa characteristic. A hoof that has vertical stripes of alternating layers of pink and black material. Some horsemen believe that a pink hoof is soft, a black one is flinty and hard, and a striped or "laminated" hoof ideally combines the tough layers between the softer cushions of the pink material.

Supple. Flexible, smooth and limber in movement.

Tack. A collection of horse equipment used for riding which includes a saddle, bridle, saddle pad or blanket, martingale and breast-collar.

Thrush. A disease of the foot that causes a thick, black discharge that has a very offensive odor from the area of the frog. It is usually caused by standing for long periods of time in dirty stalls or in urine, or in wet, marshy ground. The foot must be kept dry and treated with an astringent such as Absorbine. A vet must be called in severe cases.

Travois. The American Indian did not have or use the wheel. Instead, he would fasten two long poles (usually his teepee or wikiup poles), one on each side of a horse or dog, in the same fashion as animal is attached to the shafts of a cart or buggy. The ends of the poles would drag behind and a hide would be stretched between these two poles where possessions or people would then be supported and carried.

Varnish marks. A concentration of dark hairs that commonly occurs on the frontal bones of the horse's face, above the eye, on the point of the hip and behind the elbow of an Appaloosa horse, particularly with those that have a roan color pattern.

Veterinarian. A licensed doctor of veterinary medicine and surgery who is qualified to treat the diseases and injuries of animals such as the horse.

Weanling. When a foal is weaned and no longer nurses from its mother, usually at about five or six months of age, it is called a "weanling." A male is called a "weanling colt", and a female a "weanling filly."

Winging. An exaggerated form of "paddling" in which the horse moves his feet in large, outward arcs, causing him to move in an awkward manner.

Yearling. A colt or filly becomes a yearling on January 1 of the year following birth, regardless of his actual chronological age.

Gestation Table

Date of Service	Birth	Date of Service	Birth	Date of Service	Birth
Jan. 1	Dec. 7	Mar. 2	Feb. 5	May 2	Apr. 7
4	10	5	8	5	10
7	13	8	11	8	13
10	16	11	14	11	16
13	19	14	17	14	19
16	22	17	20	17	22
19	25	21	24	20	25
22	28	24	27	23	28
25	31	27	Mar. 2	26	May 1
28	Jan. 3	30	5	29	4
31	6			June 1	7
Feb. 3	Jan. 9	Apr. 2	Mar. 8	June 4	May 10
6	12	5	11	7	13
9	15	8	14	10	16
12	18	11	17	13	19
15	21	14	20	16	22
18	24	17	23	19	25
21	27	20	26	22	28
24	30	23	29	25	31
27	Feb. 2	26	Apr. 1	28	June 3
		29	4		
July 1	June 6	Sept. 2	Aug. 8	Nov. 3	Oct. 10
4	9	5	11	6	13
7	12	8	14	9	16
10	15	11	17	12	19
13	18	14	20	15	22
16	21	17	23	18	25
19	24	20	26	21	28
22	27	23	29	24	31
25	30	26	Sept. 1	27	Nov. 3
28	July 3	29	4	30	6
31	6				
Aug. 3	July 9	Oct. 1	Sept. 7	Dec. 3	Nov. 9
6	12	4	10	6	12
9	15	7	13	9	15
12	18	10	16	12	18
15	21	13	19	15	21
18	24	16	22	18	24
21	27	19	25	21	27
24	30	22	28	24	30
27	Aug. 2	25	Oct. 1	27	Dec. 3
30	5	28	4	30	6
		31	7		

Index

A PERSONAL WORD FROM MELVIN POWERS
PUBLISHER, WILSHIRE BOOK COMPANY

Dear Friend:

My goal is to publish interesting, informative, and inspirational books. You can help me accomplish this by answering the following questions, either by phone or by mail. Or, if convenient for you, I would welcome the opportunity to visit with you in my office and hear your comments in person.

Did you enjoy reading this book? Why?

Would you enjoy reading another similar book?

What idea in the book impressed you the most?

If applicable to your situation, have you incorporated this idea in your daily life?

Is there a chapter that could serve as a theme for an entire book? Please explain.

If you have an idea for a book, I would welcome discussing it with you. If you already have one in progress, write or call me concerning possible publication. I can be reached at **(818) 765-8579.**

Sincerely yours,

MELVIN POWERS

12015 Sherman Road
North Hollywood, California 91605

MELVIN POWERS SELF-IMPROVEMENT LIBRARY

____ HOW TO WIN AT CHECKERS *Fred Reinfeld*	5.00
____ 1001 BRILLIANT WAYS TO CHECKMATE *Fred Reinfeld*	7.00
____ 1001 WINNING CHESS SACRIFICES & COMBINATIONS *Fred Reinfeld*	7.00

COOKERY & HERBS

____ CULPEPER'S HERBAL REMEDIES *Dr. Nicholas Culpeper*	5.00
____ FAST GOURMET COOKBOOK *Poppy Cannon*	2.50
____ HEALING POWER OF HERBS *May Bethel*	5.00
____ HEALING POWER OF NATURAL FOODS *May Bethel*	5.00
____ HERBS FOR HEALTH—HOW TO GROW & USE THEM *Louise Evans Doole*	4.00
____ HOME GARDEN COOKBOOK—DELICIOUS NATURAL FOOD RECIPES *Ken Kraft*	3.00
____ MEATLESS MEAL GUIDE *Tomi Ryan & James H. Ryan, M.D.*	4.00
____ VEGETABLE GARDENING FOR BEGINNERS *Hugh Wiberg*	2.00
____ VEGETABLES FOR TODAY'S GARDENS *R. Milton Carleton*	2.00
____ VEGETARIAN COOKERY *Janet Walker*	7.00
____ VEGETARIAN COOKING MADE EASY & DELECTABLE *Veronica Vezza*	3.00
____ VEGETARIAN DELIGHTS—A HAPPY COOKBOOK FOR HEALTH *K. R. Mehta*	2.00
____ VEGETARIAN GOURMET COOKBOOK *Joyce McKinnel*	3.00

GAMBLING & POKER

____ ADVANCED POKER STRATEGY & WINNING PLAY *A. D. Livingston*	5.00
____ HOW TO WIN AT DICE GAMES *Skip Frey*	3.00
____ HOW TO WIN AT POKER *Terence Reese & Anthony T. Watkins*	7.00
____ WINNING AT CRAPS *Dr. Lloyd T. Commins*	5.00
____ WINNING AT GIN *Chester Wander & Cy Rice*	3.00
____ WINNING AT POKER—AN EXPERT'S GUIDE *John Archer*	5.00
____ WINNING AT 21—AN EXPERT'S GUIDE *John Archer*	5.00
____ WINNING POKER SYSTEMS *Norman Zadeh*	3.00

HEALTH

____ BEE POLLEN *Lynda Lyngheim & Jack Scagnetti*	3.00
____ COPING WITH ALZHEIMER'S *Rose Oliver, Ph.D. & Francis Bock, Ph.D.*	7.00
____ DR. LINDNER'S POINT SYSTEM FOOD PROGRAM *Peter G. Lindner, M.D.*	2.00
____ HELP YOURSELF TO BETTER SIGHT *Margaret Darst Corbett*	7.00
____ HOW YOU CAN STOP SMOKING PERMANENTLY *Ernest Caldwell*	5.00
____ MIND OVER PLATTER *Peter G. Lindner, M.D.*	5.00
____ NATURE'S WAY TO NUTRITION & VIBRANT HEALTH *Robert J. Scrutton*	3.00
____ NEW CARBOHYDRATE DIET COUNTER *Patti Lopez-Pereira*	2.00
____ REFLEXOLOGY *Dr. Maybelle Segal*	5.00
____ REFLEXOLOGY FOR GOOD HEALTH *Anna Kaye & Don C. Matchan*	5.00
____ 30 DAYS TO BEAUTIFUL LEGS *Dr. Marc Selner*	3.00
____ YOU CAN LEARN TO RELAX *Dr. Samuel Gutwirth*	3.00

HOBBIES

____ BEACHCOMBING FOR BEGINNERS *Norman Hickin*	2.00
____ BLACKSTONE'S MODERN CARD TRICKS *Harry Blackstone*	5.00
____ BLACKSTONE'S SECRETS OF MAGIC *Harry Blackstone*	5.00
____ COIN COLLECTING FOR BEGINNERS *Burton Hobson & Fred Reinfeld*	5.00
____ ENTERTAINING WITH ESP *Tony 'Doc' Shiels*	2.00
____ 400 FASCINATING MAGIC TRICKS YOU CAN DO *Howard Thurston*	5.00
____ HOW I TURN JUNK INTO FUN AND PROFIT *Sari*	3.00
____ HOW TO WRITE A HIT SONG & SELL IT *Tommy Boyce*	7.00
____ JUGGLING MADE EASY *Rudolf Dittrich*	3.00
____ MAGIC FOR ALL AGES *Walter Gibson*	4.00
____ MAGIC MADE EASY *Byron Wels*	2.00
____ STAMP COLLECTING FOR BEGINNERS *Burton Hobson*	3.00

HORSE PLAYER'S WINNING GUIDES

____ BETTING HORSES TO WIN *Les Conklin*	7.00
____ ELIMINATE THE LOSERS *Bob McKnight*	5.00
____ HOW TO PICK WINNING HORSES *Bob McKnight*	5.00

___	LEFT-HANDED PEOPLE *Michael Barsley*	5.00
___	MAGIC IN YOUR MIND *U.S. Andersen*	7.00
___	MAGIC OF THINKING BIG *Dr. David J. Schwartz*	3.00
___	MAGIC OF THINKING SUCCESS *Dr. David J. Schwartz*	7.00
___	MAGIC POWER OF YOUR MIND *Walter M. Germain*	7.00
___	MENTAL POWER THROUGH SLEEP SUGGESTION *Melvin Powers*	3.00
___	NEVER UNDERESTIMATE THE SELLING POWER OF A WOMAN *Dottie Walters*	7.00
___	NEW GUIDE TO RATIONAL LIVING *Albert Ellis, Ph.D. & R. Harper, Ph.D.*	7.00
___	PSYCHO-CYBERNETICS *Maxwell Maltz, M.D.*	7.00
___	PSYCHOLOGY OF HANDWRITING *Nadya Olyanova*	7.00
___	SALES CYBERNETICS *Brian Adams*	7.00
___	SCIENCE OF MIND IN DAILY LIVING *Dr. Donald Curtis*	7.00
___	SECRET OF SECRETS *U.S. Andersen*	7.00
___	SECRET POWER OF THE PYRAMIDS *U. S. Andersen*	7.00
___	SELF-THERAPY FOR THE STUTTERER *Malcolm Frazer*	3.00
___	SUCCESS-CYBERNETICS *U. S. Andersen*	7.00
___	10 DAYS TO A GREAT NEW LIFE *William E. Edwards*	3.00
___	THINK AND GROW RICH *Napoleon Hill*	7.00
___	THREE MAGIC WORDS *U. S. Andersen*	7.00
___	TREASURY OF COMFORT *Edited by Rabbi Sidney Greenberg*	7.00
___	TREASURY OF THE ART OF LIVING *Sidney S. Greenberg*	7.00
___	WHAT YOUR HANDWRITING REVEALS *Albert E. Hughes*	4.00
___	YOUR SUBCONSCIOUS POWER *Charles M. Simmons*	7.00
___	YOUR THOUGHTS CAN CHANGE YOUR LIFE *Dr. Donald Curtis*	7.00

SPORTS

___	BICYCLING FOR FUN AND GOOD HEALTH *Kenneth E. Luther*	2.00
___	BILLIARDS—POCKET • CAROM • THREE CUSHION *Clive Cottingham, Jr.*	5.00
___	COMPLETE GUIDE TO FISHING *Vlad Evanoff*	2.00
___	HOW TO IMPROVE YOUR RACQUETBALL *Lubarsky, Kaufman & Scagnetti*	5.00
___	HOW TO WIN AT POCKET BILLIARDS *Edward D. Knuchell*	7.00
___	JOY OF WALKING *Jack Scagnetti*	3.00
___	LEARNING & TEACHING SOCCER SKILLS *Eric Worthington*	3.00
___	MOTORCYCLING FOR BEGINNERS *I.G. Edmonds*	3.00
___	RACQUETBALL FOR WOMEN *Toni Hudson, Jack Scagnetti & Vince Rondone*	3.00
___	RACQUETBALL MADE EASY *Steve Lubarsky, Rod Delson & Jack Scagnetti*	5.00
___	SECRET OF BOWLING STRIKES *Dawson Taylor*	5.00
___	SECRET OF PERFECT PUTTING *Horton Smith & Dawson Taylor*	5.00
___	SOCCER—THE GAME & HOW TO PLAY IT *Gary Rosenthal*	5.00
___	STARTING SOCCER *Edward F. Dolan, Jr.*	5.00

TENNIS LOVER'S LIBRARY

___	BEGINNER'S GUIDE TO WINNING TENNIS *Helen Hull Jacobs*	2.00
___	HOW TO BEAT BETTER TENNIS PLAYERS *Loring Fiske*	4.00
___	PSYCH YOURSELF TO BETTER TENNIS *Dr. Walter A. Luszki*	2.00
___	TENNIS FOR BEGINNERS *Dr. H. A. Murray*	2.00
___	TENNIS MADE EASY *Joel Brecheen*	5.00
___	WEEKEND TENNIS—HOW TO HAVE FUN & WIN AT THE SAME TIME *Bill Talbert*	3.00

WILSHIRE PET LIBRARY

___	DOG OBEDIENCE TRAINING *Gust Kessopulos*	5.00
___	DOG TRAINING MADE EASY & FUN *John W. Kellogg*	5.00
___	HOW TO BRING UP YOUR PET DOG *Kurt Unkelbach*	2.00
___	HOW TO RAISE & TRAIN YOUR PUPPY *Jeff Griffen*	5.00

The books listed above can be obtained from your book dealer or directly from Melvin Powers. When ordering, please remit $1.50 postage for the first book and 50¢ for each additional book.

Melvin Powers
12015 Sherman Road, No. Hollywood, California 91605